THE OLD STONE AGE

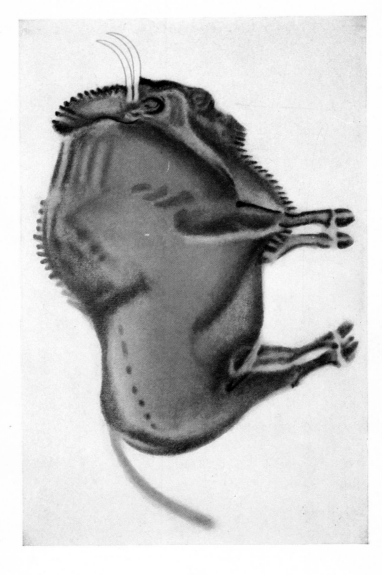

Polychrome cave painting (phase D) on the ceiling at Altamira.

THE OLD STONE AGE

A STUDY OF PALAEOLITHIC TIMES

by

M. C. BURKITT, M.A., F.S.A., F.G.S.

University Lecturer in the Faculty of Archaeology and
Anthropology in the University of Cambridge

Author of

*Prehistory, Our Early Ancestors, South Africa's
Past in Stone and Paint*

Third Edition

NEW YORK UNIVERSITY PRESS

Washington Square   New York

First edition published by Cambridge University Press 1933
Second edition 1949
Third edition, Bowes & Bowes Publishers, London, 1955
First United States edition 1956

Library of Congress catalogue card number: 56-10678

Printed in the United States of America

PREFACE TO THIRD EDITION

IS prehistoric archaeology to be classed as a science or as a humanity? The question has often been asked and the answer is, of course, as both. The student is indeed concerned with early man himself, but the methods he uses to obtain information are scientific—mainly geological, though of recent years the physical sciences have been increasingly employed. But scientific methods can only deal with facts and tangible things, and it is only man's handiwork that has survived from prehistoric times that can be accurately studied; many sides of human experience must necessarily remain matters for speculation. We can determine what kind of implements belong to a particular culture and how they were made; we can even assert with confidence that the economy of the Magdalenians was based on reindeer; but we can know nothing about the personal life of these ancient folk, and can never give a complete picture of life in prehistoric times such as is possible in the case of modern primitive peoples whose institutions and ways of life can be studied. Speculations based on the assumption that similar circumstances engender similar outlooks on life, and that, therefore, what can be learnt from the study of modern primitive cultures can be applied piecemeal to prehistoric studies can be dangerous. Those who come fresh to the subject should, at any rate at first, treat it rigidly as a science. This book is intended for beginners and the approach is, therefore, purely scientific and as far as possible speculations have been eschewed. I have had a long experience in teaching the subject and I feel strongly that this is the proper

20956

course, even if as a result the picture given remains incomplete. More particularly should lower palaeolithic man and his cultures be treated as fossils. In the case of upper palaeolithic and mesolithic man—our forerunners—perhaps it is legitimate to infer more. But it is only with the neolithic civilisation that we can consider man as our cultural ancestor whose outlook on life can begin to be compared with our own.

I have made few fundamental changes in this edition. But I have made some additions and alterations to bring the volume as far as possible up to date.

Perhaps this is the best place in which to say one word of warning as regards the painted caves in France and Spain. Where these have been exploited for the tourist the alternations of temperature and humidity consequent on the passage through them of thousands of visitors have caused erosion of the walls and the paintings are starting to disappear. Anyone wishing to see this wonderful art should take an early opportunity to do so. I can personally vouch for the fact that at some sites much has vanished since 1912.

Once again I welcome the opportunity of putting on record my sense of obligation to my former "gurus" Professor Breuil and the late Dr Obermaier. The pictures in this book illustrating the upper palaeolithic art are for the most part ultimately derived from tracings made by the former, and he has always generously allowed me to copy any of his published work. The Editor of *The Illustrated London News* has most kindly allowed me to reproduce as Plate I an original reconstruction drawing by the late M. Forestier which represents life in a rock-shelter as it must have been. For permission to make and reproduce the photograph of the Venus of Unter Wisternitz I am delighted to thank

Dr Absolon: in connection with the photographs of the
Venus of Lespugue M. de St Périer and M. Vaufrey,
Editor of *L'Anthropologie*: and for that of the sculpture
from Le Roc Dr Lantier, Editor of *Préhistoire*—the not
too well-known and important periodical whose appearance all prehistorians have welcomed: and also Mrs W.
Hemp for valuable help in connection with the cave art
superposition drawings. My wife has helped me in
correcting the proofs and making the index and has also
made the drawings of the implements, etc.

M. C. BURKITT

MERTON HOUSE
GRANTCHESTER
1954

CONTENTS

THE OLD STONE AGE

Chapter I

INTRODUCTION

THE terms prehistory, prehistorian, prehistoric are strictly speaking misnomers: there is no period before history begins: the geologist is concerned with the history of the earth long before mankind was ever evolved, and so to call a subject prehistory would at first sight appear absurd. However, the use of the terms has become established in modern speech and literature; they have come to represent something that everybody understands, and as there are no more scientific expressions to replace them it would be absurd and pedantic to attempt to make a change now. Prehistory, then, is the subject which deals with the story of man and everything that concerns him from that dim remote moment when he first emerged from his animal ancestry until the time when the existence of written records leads the investigator into the realm of history proper. Those archaeologists who principally concern themselves with the end of the prehistoric period when contact with history is being made, but before literary history unassisted by the spade can really carry on the story, are sometimes known as proto-historians, and their subject, protohistory.

Obviously the extent of time covered by the prehistorian is immense. The prehistoric period during which early cultures and civilisations were laboriously evolved, rose, and fell may well have occupied more than a million years; the student must not therefore expect in one short volume more than an outline of the history of this vast period—for the amazing thing is how much actually has been learned of the ways of life, ideas and migrations of these immensely ancient populations. Neither the lower nor the upper time limits of the subject can be strictly defined. It will probably always be very difficult to say exactly when we can correctly talk about humanity as such. The development from the animal state was probably a gradual mental process and it is therefore almost impossible to draw a hard and fast line at any moment. That humanity must have crossed a "Rubicon" in emerging from the animal state is obvious, but how best to define this Rubicon has puzzled many minds. For some the kindling of fire, probably soon afterwards followed by the cooking of food, has been the touchstone which distinguishes the human kind from their animal forbears; for others man is the first tool-using animal; while for others again— I fancy Dr Elliot Smith would have been among the number—it is the development of the speech areas in the brain which makes the difference. Others again have stressed the assumption of the erect attitude, but this physical change would itself seem to be rather the result of a mental evolution, a symptom rather than a cause. It is equally difficult to define accurately the upper time limit, and this for the simple reason that it varies very widely in different geographical regions. The prehistoric period, for example, came to an end at a much earlier date in Egypt than it did in Lapland. Again we have information from written documents about the great Bronze Age civilisation of the Aegean that takes us back several thousand years to a time when our knowledge of Great Britain could still only be obtained through methods employed by the prehistorian.

In other parts of the world this difference in the upper limit is still more marked. In South Africa, for example, it cannot be fixed any earlier than the seventeenth century of our era, and indeed many people would say that even then the information obtained from written records is so meagre as hardly to count before the nineteenth century.

It will be obvious too that it has become impossible to describe within the limits of a single volume anything in the nature of a world prehistory, and indeed it will soon be beyond the powers of any single individual to master the whole of such a far-flung study except in its broadest outline. Between the two world wars information on prehistoric subjects all over the world had been and still is accumulating apace, and therefore, when writing a book, the author must necessarily confine himself within certain limits, both regionally and in time. For the purposes of this volume, then, the area covered will be primarily restricted to Europe and the neighbouring countries in so far as they affect its pre-history; while in time, though starting at the very beginning, the subject will not be pursued much further than the end of that great major period of prehistory which is known as the palaeolithic or Old Stone Age.

But before embarking on this study of our area it will be necessary to spend some time in discussing the preliminaries of the subject and the methods employed by the prehistorian to obtain his information. Pre-history as a science is still young[1] and, like many other

[1] It would seem that the first stone implement recognised as such was discovered as long ago as 1690 during the course of an excavation in Gray's Inn Lane, London. It was considered to be Roman in date. A hundred years later, however, Frere, the real father of prehistory, noticed in a brick-earth pit at Hoxne, Suffolk, the association of flint implements with

scientific youngsters, biochemistry for example, it has carved out its inheritance as it were from those of a number of other related sciences. But while relationships with these scientific sponsors should never be forgotten, and while it is perfectly correct to stress the fact that strictly speaking no subject can be really independent, that all branches of study—especially when they refer to a single object such as man—are interconnected, yet it cannot be too strongly urged that prehistory must now be considered as a distinct and grown-up subject, existing independently of its former guardians. Moreover, in the last few years it has itself developed to such an amazing extent that we may even talk about its own dependents, distinct branches of prehistory. Naturally an ultraspecialist, concerned only with a single subdivision of the subject, can seldom, if ever, get a general view of the whole new edifice of knowledge: he is, as it were, a bricklayer doing nothing but adding brick to brick in one wing of the building, and when, as in this generation, so many bricks are to hand, he should hardly be disturbed in his all-important work. His function is not to step back and view the

the bones of extinct animals. Such associations were further demonstrated in rock-shelters by Tournal at Bize, near Narbonne, in France, and by Schmerling in Belgium. In 1859 Evans and Prestwich visited Boucher de Perthes at Abbeville and were convinced that certain stone implements were contemporary with the gravels of the river terraces of pleistocene age in which they had there been found. Since that date the scientific world has accepted the idea of pleistocene man, although there are still some prehistorians who cannot admit his existence at a still earlier date. While prehistoric home art had been recognised for some time (actually the first discovery, which was at the time thought to be of Celtic age, was made at the cave of Chaffaud (Vienne) as long ago as 1834) the authenticity of the cave art was only admitted as recently as 1895, and it is to the first decade of this century that the discoveries of most of the painted caves belong.

building as it is arising, to examine the lay-out, to notice the co-ordination of the parts. But there is room for such an observer; indeed he is a necessity, and in many ways his is the more difficult task. From time to time he should come forward and, for the sake of the student starting to take an interest in the subject, he should try to give a general and connected account of the building as a whole or at least of some major aspect of it which is of special interest.

In its earlier phases prehistory is very closely related to geology; indeed, it was at one time considered as a branch of quaternary geology. Moreover, as will appear a little later, many of the methods employed by the prehistorian to obtain information are those used by the geologist. Another closely allied subject is anthropology, or more strictly speaking ethnology. Modern primitive peoples living to-day under natural uncivilised conditions by no means lead simple and unsophisticated lives. Their customs and institutions are frequently very complex, and by analogy there is no reason to believe that the life of prehistoric man throughout much of the period covered by the prehistorian was any less developed and elaborate. From the ethnologist, therefore, who studies modern primitive peoples living under somewhat similar conditions much information can be obtained and used to fill in gaps in the story of prehistoric man. Naturally the greatest discrimination must be used in this respect; but since in the nature of the case our only information about his way of life and activities is what we can deduce from a study of his indestructible possessions which have survived from the dim past till now, there would be whole chapters of his story which could never be written, or even guessed at, without the help of ethnological comparisons.

Psychology, too, is important. It seems probable that man as a thinking being has changed but little during immense periods of time. Real progress is not concerned with the mere harnessing of natural forces, with discoveries such as those of steam and wireless. It is of a far more intangible, perhaps even "spiritual", nature. In the past civilisations have arisen and fallen, material prosperity has grown and waned, desires have arisen and found their fulfilment, but the thread of real progress which many of us believe does exist is hard to follow and difficult to define. It would appear, then, that if real change in human mental progress is so gradual, information obtained to-day by the psychologist through study and experiment will be to a large measure applicable to prehistoric man during, at any rate, much of our period, and so it is necessary that the prehistorian should not neglect what the psychologist may have to offer from this point of view. Finally, it occasionally happens, alas all too rarely, that the remains of prehistoric man himself are discovered. The study of human skeletons is clearly a task for the anatomist, and so specialised is this work that it is seldom wise for the prehistorian, unless specially equipped for the purpose, to attempt it. None the less the study of comparative anatomy from the point of view of prehistoric skeletons strictly speaking falls within the province of the prehistorian, and while as yet, owing to the paucity of available material, results of any value are still but meagre—perhaps of less importance than some comparative anatomists would like us to think—as more and more material comes to hand in the course of the next few decades it will probably be found that more definite data will become available to help in the writing of the story of man's physical evolution.

So much for the major allied sciences. We turn now to considerations of the prehistorian's own peculiar province. Most of our information about palaeolithic man results from the excavation of his "homes". These are of two kinds: (i) cave or rock-shelter homes, and (ii) open stations.

(i) The expression "cave man" is somewhat misleading; our prehistoric forerunners never lived in the depths of their caves. For one thing caves are very damp and rheumatism seems to have been as rife then as it is now; furthermore, they would have required perpetual artificial light. They did, however, frequently inhabit the mouths of caves where these were not too draughty, but seem to have preferred situations under overhanging cliffs where natural differential weathering had produced rock-shelters. Such rock-shelters, situated on the sunny side of a valley above a stream which ensured a plentiful water-supply and whence a good outlook for observing both enemies and game could be obtained, must have been not unpleasant or uncomfortable places (Plate I). Doubtless before the front of the rock-shelter skins would have been hung or a protection of some other material erected to keep out the cold. To-day in France, in the hamlet of Giroteaux in the Dordogne, just such rock-shelters are still inhabited, there being merely one built wall with doorways and windows blocking up the front.[1]

(ii) Open stations, as their name implies, are merely settlement sites in the open. As a rule they were situated near a river or water of some kind, and it would seem natural to suppose that they simply consisted of small wigwam-like shelters made of some perishable material which has now completely disappeared. The inhabitants of these shelters naturally threw away the bones of the animals they had eaten, their broken or discarded tools

[1] Such rock-houses are also still inhabited in the red sandstone of Worcestershire near the village of Wolverley.

and so on near the site, and these have sometimes become incorporated in the gravels or other deposits that were being laid down in the neighbourhood. It is these more permanent relics that the excavator occasionally finds to-day. It will be seen later on that these two different kinds of home sites, the cave-mouth or rock-shelter home and the open station, are both important to the prehistorian in his researches, but for different purposes. The one enables him to map out the sequence of events that have taken place, the other helps him to attempt a correlation of this sequence with that obtained by the geologist—in other words, a correlation of the archaeological and geological records.

When an excavation is undertaken in a home site of the first kind, say in western France, implements of various sorts and shapes are discovered. In palaeolithic times these consisted almost wholly of stone implements, or tools made of bone, antler and ivory. Further, the charred remains of hearths are found, the fireplaces round which prehistoric man sat and cooked his food. The bones of the animals that he ate occur in profusion, and these frequently belong to a fauna now extinct from the world altogether,[1] or only living in far distant areas under climatic conditions quite different from those obtaining at the prehistoric site to-day.

The list on the next page enumerates the more important of these animals which were familiar to palaeolithic man at various times.

Apart from other proofs derived directly from geological considerations, it will be seen from a perusal of

[1] It may be noted in passing that the bones found in the homes are frequently split longitudinally—doubtless for the purpose of extracting the marrow. Man is the only animal who thus breaks bones, his tongue being too short to suck out the marrow as do other animals who either gnaw off the ends or break them transversely.

this list of fauna that the climate of western Europe was not by any means uniform throughout palaeolithic times. Naturally this fact had a vital effect on the

Name	Climatic conditions or type of country preferred
Felis spelæa, the cave lion (extinct)	Relatively warm
Elephas antiquus, the straight-tusked elephant (extinct)	,,
Hippopotamus major, the hippopotamus	,,
Rhinoceros Merckii, the soft-nosed rhinoceros (extinct)	,,
Machairodus (several species), the sabre-toothed tiger (extinct)	,,
Cervus megaceros, the giant deer (extinct)	Forest country
Cervus capreolus caprea, the roebuck	,,
Castor fiber, the beaver	,,
Sus scrofa ferus, the wild boar	,,
Equus caballus ferus, the wild horse	Open country
Cervus elaphus, the red deer	,,
Canis lupus, the wolf	,,
Bos priscus, the bison	Steppe country
Bos primigenius, the aurochs (extinct)	,,
Antilope saiga, the saïga	,,
Arvicola (several species), the voles	,,
Elephas primigenius, the mammoth (extinct)	Arctic tundra
Rhinoceros tichorhinus, the woolly rhinoceros (extinct)	,,
Ovibos moschatus, the musk ox	,,
Ursus spelæus, the cave bear (extinct)	,,
Cervus tarandus, the reindeer	,,
Canis lagopus, the arctic fox	,,
Lepus variabilis, the variable hare	,,
Myodes torquatus, the banded lemming	,,

human story, and the matter will have to be considered in some detail in due course. The student should never forget that changes of climate do not consist only in changes of temperature; almost as important are changes in humidity: both these factors influence life. For example, some animals can stand great changes of temperature but are rather sensitive to changes of humidity and *vice versa*. Again, a distinction must be made between herb-eating and flesh-eating animals; the latter will often stand extreme changes of climate as long as there are animals to prey upon, but the former, dependent as they are on certain kinds of plant life, are much more liable to be affected if the grasses or mosses that they require for food succumb to altered conditions. When this happens they either die out themselves or migrate to other regions where the climate is more suitable for the growth of the particular food they like. It follows, then, that fauna can only be used as indicators of climate with discrimination, and indeed it is not so much the presence or absence of any given species but the general assemblage of species, and above all the proportion in which they occur, that must be taken into consideration. For example, it may be noted that throughout the cold period, known as the reindeer age, in late palaeolithic times, remains of red deer are almost always present, but the proportion of red deer to reindeer is very small, and the general assemblage of animals indicates that the climate was far colder than that obtaining in the same region to-day.

As is always the case with a new branch of learning, a sort of jargon has grown up in which new words have been coined or more frequently old words have come to be used with a definite connotation. Before going farther, then, it might be well to set forth a few simple definitions. It cannot be too strongly urged that care should be used in the employment of these terms and that they should not be thought of as synonyms for one another.

ARTIFACT. The word artifact is used to include all objects made or fashioned by prehistoric man. Tools used in the home, weapons required for hunting, engraved or sculptured objects, are all artifacts; so too, when they occur, are fragments of pottery, beads, pierced shells or teeth, such as were doubtless used strung together as necklaces, though the latter, together with other objects of decoration, may be more particularly classed as ornaments.

INDUSTRY. An assemblage of artifacts at a given site, when all are of the same age, is described as the industry of that site. Should a site have been inhabited at successive periods, there being in consequence more than one assemblage of artifacts belonging respectively to several different ages, then several different industries are said to occur.

CULTURE. Naturally industries of the same age in widely separated districts, even when made by the same race of people, are not absolutely identical. Many types of tools, however, will be common throughout and there will be an evident connection between them. A culture, then, denotes in the first place an assemblage of industries made by people of the same stock. But besides this merely material definition something further is included in the word culture when used by the prehistorian which perhaps is particularly connoted by the German word *kultur*; something more abstract that gives us an idea of the way of life and mental outlook of the people with whom we are concerned. In making a description of a culture, therefore, it is necessary to take into account not only the various industries which occur but also any other factor, such as art, burial customs, etc., which will help us to discover anything of the life and minds of the people themselves. It will be noticed that in defining the term culture there are introduced for the first time the words people and stock. In the case of artifacts, or industries, we are only concerned with the objects themselves and not with the people who made them. When we talk about a culture we are not only concerned with the relics but also with the people who have left us those relics.

CIVILISATION. A civilisation denotes a larger unit than a culture and it may comprise a number of quite independent cultures, the connection between them not being necessarily racial but rather the conditions and mode of life obtaining. Thus we can talk of a hunter stage of civilisation as distinct from the stage when man became a grower of crops, or again, when the domestication of animals was being practised we may talk of a herdsman or nomad stage. The kind of life developed by man in early days was very largely the result of the climatic conditions under which he had to live, and this naturally varied in different areas and at different times. To some extent, then, particular civilisations can be thought of as functions of particular climates; but clearly this line of thought can be carried too far and, while man may be a far more automatic animal and more subject to natural conditions surrounding him than he sometimes likes to imagine, there are plenty of factors besides the climatic ones that tend to modify the mode of life which he develops at any given time and in any given place.

CULTURAL AND TIME SEQUENCES. The student must always remember that when an artifact or industry is compared with similar finds in another district, or part of the world, no connection between them is necessarily implied; as has just been said, like conditions, climatic and otherwise, engender to a very large extent like requirements and as a result the production of similar types of tools. Is not the same necessity the mother of the same invention? When, however, two industries are said to belong to the same culture, a connection between the folk producing them is denoted although no contemporaneity in age is necessarily implied. This latter point should be clearly grasped. The same culture may occur in one part of the world at a given time and in a vastly different area at another time. Thus we can say with a fair surety that in old stone age times the same culture is found both in South Africa and western Europe, but that does not mean to say that the two are strictly contemporaneous; there may indeed be several hundreds of years between them. The culture in the one country may be the result of a migration from the other, and that may have taken a very long time. Furthermore we may often find that a given culture exhibits an evolution within itself that can be represented by A to B to C, and that this evolution can be demonstrated in two widely separated areas. Here again, there is no reason to suggest that A in both areas is contemporary; indeed the opposite is likely, and it is quite as probable that A of one area will be contemporary with B of the other. It follows, then, that when dealing with cultures and cultural sequences in different areas the time factor is not taken into account unless on other grounds it can be demonstrated.[1] A typological study of the industries can tell us little as to their contemporaneity; to demonstrate this latter it is necessary that they should be found in similar geological deposits which on other grounds can be shown to be of the same age.

[1] But probably only seldom should any vast time-lag be postulated.

The work of the prehistorian in the last fifty years has demonstrated a succession of cultures occurring in Europe during prehistoric times, this succession forming a chronological sequence. But recently it has become abundantly clear that even in the different parts of such a small area as Europe the observable changes in the cultures are not invariably uniform and due solely to the time factor; but that problems of geographical distribution have to be taken into account. The succession of cultures, as determined in western France by a long line of brilliant investigators starting with Gabriel de Mortillet, need not necessarily, and in fact does not, hold good when we pass on into central Europe. It would seem, then, that already as early as old stone age times some racial differentiation of peoples had already taken place and any rigid application of a chronological scheme of culture-sequences which can be proved true for western Europe will not necessarily be applicable in other areas hard by. It cannot be too strongly urged that the student should clearly understand what has just been said. Many difficulties that have arisen of late years are simply due to the fact that this problem of the geographical distribution of completely different though contemporary cultures has not been realised. The prehistory of different areas must be worked out by local prehistorians independently, and only afterwards can cultural and time correlations with other countries be attempted. Some prehistoric peoples seem to have evolved fairly uniformly in culture throughout long periods of time and in widely separated parts of the world, others seem continually to have been experimenting, to have been evolving in different regions slightly differing industrial characteristics. In the latter case the varying cultures produced are grouped together as a culture-complex. Clearly the cultures within such a complex are more closely connected with one another than they are with those belonging to another culture-complex—just as the fingers of one hand are more closely connected to one another than they are to the fingers of the other hand, though ultimately all part of one organism.

In this connection it is not out of place to say a word about the vexed question of inter-cultural influence. In a small area such as Europe it is quite obvious that two different cultures cannot have existed in prehistoric times side by side without there having been culture contact, at any rate along the line of junction between them. We therefore should expect, and in many cases do find, if not true hybrids, at least developments of one culture showing influences from the other; and even beyond the actual geographical line of junction, the influence of one may spread somewhat into the territory of the other—there may be even an actual interchange through trade or otherwise of a certain number of tools, etc., far beyond the limits actually reached by the people who made them. All this seems very up-to-date, the sort of thing we find in the modern world of to-day, but the more we study prehistoric times the more we find that while life was much simpler and while transport was much slower and more restricted, yet in some ways comparisons with modern conditions are not out of place. But there will be more to be said on this matter later on when we come to deal in detail with the story of palaeolithic Europe.

Chapter II

METHODS OF STUDY

THERE are four main lines along which prehistoric studies are pursued. These involve respectively considerations of (i) Stratigraphy, (ii) Typology and Technology, (iii) the Associated Finds and (iv) the State of Preservation of the Artifacts.

STRATIGRAPHY. The stratigraphical method of approach to the subject depends on the geological law of superposition. This states that in the case of deposits resulting from aggradation (i.e. building up by deposition) and where there has been no subsequent disturbance, the lower beds are successively older than the upper ones: that is to say that the top level is of more recent formation than the one it rests on, which in its turn is newer than the one just below and so on, the bottom layer being of course the oldest of all. Let us see how the prehistorian can apply this law in the case of a cave or rock-shelter site. Let us imagine such a site to have become tenanted by a prehistoric family, and that for thousands of years afterwards it continues to be so occupied.

The first-comers will be making their home on the natural floor of the rock-shelter, but as time passes and one generation follows another, the floor level will become covered with material partly fallen from the roof and walls, partly introduced from outside in the form of mud and dirt and so on by the occupants themselves, and partly made up of the actual materials, such as broken bones, tools, etc., which they throw on one side. Again, the cinders of the hearth will accumulate and add to the growth of the deposit. The descendants or successors of the original newcomers will be living on the top of this deposit and adding in their turn a fresh layer of accumulating débris. When slight changes in climate or otherwise are taking place or the situation of the hearth is being altered and so on, it frequently happens that the new layer may have a different consistency, or be made of different materials, or be of a different colour from its predecessor. When this is the case the excavator is indeed content, as he can thus easily divide off his layers at sight instead of having to work by a sort of dead reckoning—a circumstance which is especially helpful, as of course the layers are not all necessarily horizontal. When excavating the deposits he is thus, as it were, dealing with a pile of separate carpets laid one on top of another and his work becomes simplified, as it is only necessary to strip them off carpet by carpet, the divisions between each being clearly defined. So matters go on from generation to generation until the floor level stands much higher than it did at first, and indeed in some cases so high that the rock-shelter becomes no longer suitable for habitation—it is nearly filled up and is finally abandoned.

Clearly, the filling of the rock-shelter, as has been outlined, is due to a process of aggradation or building up, and the prehistorian, if he cuts a section through it, showing all the various layers from top to bottom, will be able to apply the geological law of superposition which has been stated above. It will follow, then, that the bottom layer will be the oldest, the middle layers intermediate, and the top layer the most recent. Naturally all this is only applied common-sense, but how much of natural science is!

Now, as has already been stated, prehistoric man frequently dropped his artifacts, and these became incorporated in the various strata; and a collection of such artifacts embedded in a single layer during the time of its formation comprises the industry of that stratum. It follows as a corollary that a complete excavation will not only enable the prehistorian to determine the sequence of strata but also a sequence of industries. No further information in this direction can be obtained at any one site, but where several excavations in one district have been undertaken, and a number of sequences of industries made out, comparison between the results obtained will enable the prehistorian to characterise the assemblages of industries of successive dates, and thus he will have gone far towards the determination of the sequence of cultures in his region. It should be noted carefully, however, that a single excavation does no more than determine the sequence of strata at a given site, and the sequence of industries, which follows as a corollary. The sequence of cultures can only be determined by comparing the results of a number of separate excavations.

In the law of superposition there is the caveat, "if there has been no subsequent disturbance". In this connection the geologist usually means earth movement; he has often to deal with the succession of strata of incredible antiquity deposited during immense periods, in the course of which slow bendings and local crackings of the earth's crust have often taken place— to say nothing of possible earthquakes or volcanic action. Such earth movements, however, do not as a rule disturb the prehistorian. The cave deposits are on too small a scale and the time since they were laid down, geologically speaking, is so inconsiderable that this particular trouble fortunately does not concern him. On the other hand, humbler, but none the less devastating agents of disturbance, are frequently present in the shape of burrowing animals, especially of course rabbits. Unless the rock-shelter deposits happen to have been sealed in at the top by some resistant material such as stalagmite (a hard, compact, limey substance, which is sometimes formed during a damp period from the redeposition on the floor of the limestone forming the walls of the rock-shelters), rabbits often drive their burrows right through them, with the result that the artifacts frequently get displaced and the industries consequently become mixed.

The most important cave site yet excavated is that of Castillo, above Puente Viesgo, a small village on the railway line from Santander to Ontañeda in North Spain (Plate II). The cave opens about half-way up the side of a rather isolated conical hill of carboniferous limestone. From it a most splendid view is obtained dominating the valley below with the river and the little village of Puente Viesgo in the bottom. Through Puente Viesgo runs a geological fault which has been responsible for a series of hot springs which there bubble up close to the river. These to-day have been enclosed, as they have been found suitable for medicinal purposes and the village of Puente Viesgo is much frequented in the summer by the bourgeoisie of Santander who go there to do a "cure". But these springs were no doubt equally popular with wild animals, and it would seem that from very early times the cave mouth at Castillo must have been very suitable for human habitation, commanding as it does the hot springs and river below with the consequently assured supply of water and game—surely an important consideration, which would mean that the hunter would not need to pursue the chase far afield, the hunted would come to him. Whether this be the correct explanation or no, Castillo was certainly inhabited off and on from very early times until the New Stone Age or neolithic period.

When the site was first discovered by prehistorians, it appeared as a low rock-shelter where a normal sized person could not stand upright. But as stratum after stratum of material was excavated, the site was found to be of immense depth and over 40 feet of deposits had to be dug away before bed-rock was reached. Layer after layer was carefully removed and the artifacts it contained studied, and it was found that practically a complete succession of cultures as far as was then known was represented.

Moreover, the prehistorian has been lucky at Castillo from another point of view. Apparently the site was several times abandoned for short periods when, for various reasons, it became too damp. Consequently deposition continued slowly to take place as a result of purely natural agencies with which man had nothing to do, and layers devoid of artifacts were laid down. These, however, sometimes contained the bones of wild animals who happened to retire to the site, perhaps to die, or who at any rate suffered some accident there, their bones remaining to be incorporated in the sterile layer, sterile, that is, so far as the works of man are concerned. These sterile layers act like blank pages in a book; they separate clearly that which has gone before from that which comes afterwards. Where one archaeological layer rests directly upon another, as so frequently happens, there naturally is a certain amount of inter-mixture at the junction of the two; there is no reason to think that prehistoric man trod delicately for the

PLATE I

A reconstruction of a prehistoric rock-shelter scene.

sake of future prehistorians! Far from it. He kicked up the ground on which he was walking together with the artifacts of his predecessors contained in it, and these became incorporated in the lower part of the levels that were being deposited while he was living and which he himself was helping to form. But where sterile layers occur at intervals, there is no such intermixture, and at Castillo we are lucky enough to have a number of them present. Furthermore, after the cave was abandoned, recurring damp conditions lead to the formation of stalagmite, and the whole deposit had been sealed in in such a way that burrowing animals have not been able subsequently to disturb it. A diagrammatic section showing this succession will be found on page 22.

The names on the left hand side of the table refer to the materials of which the different sterile layers were composed; those on the right hand side indicate the cultures to which it has been found possible, in the light of knowledge obtained from a number of other excavations, to allocate the various industries there present. The names of the cultures are derived from those of various localities in France where each was first recognised, thus:

The *Azilian* is named after the great cave at Mas d'Azil in the Pyrenees where industries belonging to this post-palaeolithic (mesolithic) culture were first unearthed from a deposit on the left bank of the stream, just before it plunges into the hill-side to form the natural tunnel of Mas d'Azil.

The *Magdalenian* is so called after the rock-shelter of La Madeleine which is to be found low down on the right bank of the River Vezère, a tributary of the Dordogne, opposite the Château of Marsac a few miles above the village of Les Eyzies.

Sterile layers	Section at Castillo	Cultures

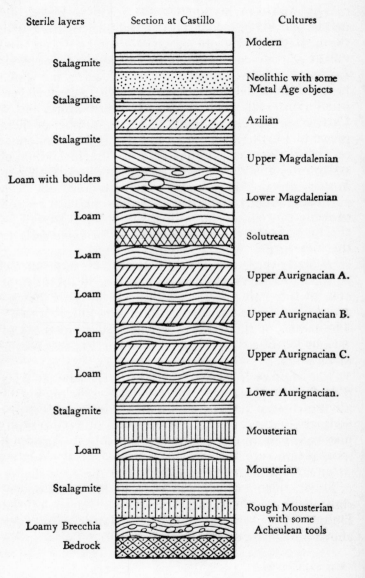

Sterile layers (left column):
- Stalagmite
- Stalagmite
- Stalagmite
- Loam with boulders
- Loam
- Loam
- Loam
- Loam
- Loam
- Stalagmite
- Loam
- Stalagmite
- Loamy Brecchia
- Bedrock

Cultures (right column):
- Modern
- Neolithic with some Metal Age objects
- Azilian
- Upper Magdalenian
- Lower Magdalenian
- Solutrean
- Upper Aurignacian A.
- Upper Aurignacian B.
- Upper Aurignacian C.
- Lower Aurignacian.
- Mousterian
- Mousterian
- Rough Mousterian with some Acheulean tools

The *Solutrean* commemorates Solutré, where the culture was first recognised in a large rock-shelter which opens at the end of an isolated hill not far from the village of that name in the department of Saône-et-Loire, not so far from Mâcon.

The *Aurignacian* is named after a small rock-shelter called Aurignac which existed near St Gaudens, in the Pyrenees district, but which has now been completely quarried away.

The *Mousterian* is so called after a rock-shelter in the village of Le Moustier some ten miles or so above Les Eyzies.

The *Acheulean* is derived from St Acheul, a suburb of Amiens, where beds in the gravel terraces bordering the River Somme have for many years yielded rich industries of this culture.

A majority of the cultures that have been recognised in western Europe occurred at Castillo, with the exception of the earlier stages of the Acheulean which are generally called Chellean[1] (from gravel pits at Chelles-sur-Marne) and certain still earlier industries which will be considered later on. Naturally, as the cultures themselves persisted for long periods, they are often subdivisible and, as will be seen from reference to the section, some, though by no means all, such subdivisions were present at Castillo. The industries belonging to the different subdivisions of a culture are naturally closely allied to one another and it is generally possible to recognise in them some sort of evolution from a more primitive to a more evolved type.

The student reading the above account of the finds at Castillo will have begun to realise how an archaeological record has been obtained; but although the site was the richest known so far, it was by no means com-

[1] Nowadays frequently called Abbevillian. Little true Chellean occurs at Chelles!

plete. It will be advisable therefore at this stage to leave as it were the actual field work and consider the complete archaeological record as pieced together from information obtained from all the various digs that have been so far made.

As long ago as 1836 Thomsen (a Danish prehistorian) suggested a threefold division for human history and prehistory. The human story could, he said, be told in three volumes, the latest, which has not yet been completed, covering the period since the use of iron for tool-making purposes was introduced. The middle volume is concerned with the time before iron came into general use, but when the smelting of copper and the alloying of it with tin to make bronze had been discovered. The first volume, with the earlier part of which we are concerned in this book, deals with a time before anything was known of metal, and when all artifacts had to be fashioned from such substances as stone, flint, bone, horn, antler, ivory, etc., and doubtless also, although it has not been preserved for us, from wood. This first volume is again subdivisible into four parts, during the last of which, the neolithic or New Stone Age, although the use of metal was still unknown, agriculture, domestic animals and pottery-making had become common. Separated from the neolithic age by the mesolithic period was the earlier and far longest portion of the first volume—the palaeolithic or Old Stone Age, with which we are here concerned. This deals with the time before agriculture or the domestication of animals was practised. Man was in the food-gathering not the food-producing stage; he was still a hunter only, not yet a herdsman or a farmer, and in the deposits of Castillo we have already seen something of the kind of material he has left behind for us to study. Still earlier even there was another period, about which unfortunately we know all too little, but which has been called "eolithic" (from *eos* = dawn and *lithos* = stone).

The following table will perhaps make this whole succession of cultures clear:

Steel and Iron	Variously subdivisible			
Bronze and Copper	Variously subdivisible			
Stone	Neolithic or New Stone Age	Subdivisible into a number of cultures		
	Mesolithic	Subdivisible into a number of cultures		
	Palaeolithic or Old Stone Age	Upper palaeolithic	Magdalenian Solutrean Aurignacian	
		Middle palaeolithic	Mousterian	Late Levalloisian Late Clactonian Tayacian
		Lower palaeolithic	Acheulean Chellean or Abbevillian	Mid and Early Levalloisian Mid and Early Clactonian Cromerian
	Eolithic			

For the sake of simplicity the various subdivisions of the cultures have been omitted; these will be mentioned in due course when the cultures themselves are described.

So far we have been solely concerned with compiling the archaeological record, and this perhaps is one of the most important contributions to knowledge that the prehistorian has made. Instead of a chaos of cultures there is now order, but it must be remembered, as has been said previously, that this archaeological record is only strictly applicable to western Europe. The major subdivisions, iron, bronze, stone, have a very wide, perhaps world-wide, application. Again, it seems likely that almost everywhere the food-gathering stage preceded that of food producing, or in other words a palaeolithic stage antedated the neolithic civilisation. On the other hand, the sequence of cultures outlined as occurring within the limits of palaeolithic times has a more restricted distribution, and the subdivisions of these cultures again a more local distribution still. Geographical considerations must now be taken into account. At the same time with this caveat the above table can be treated as a general standard, more particularly as our chief concern will be with the areas where it holds good, for the simple reason that it is in them that most exploration work has been done.

TYPOLOGY.[1] A sequence of cultures having been obtained, the prehistorian's next task is to study in detail the various industries belonging to them, and in doing this he must have recourse to considerations of typology. Typology is concerned with the classification of artifacts, and just as the stratigrapher attempts to make order out of a welter of cultures, so the typologist tries to classify all the various implements into groups or families. For this purpose two methods may be followed, or rather, more strictly speaking, two considerations must be always kept in mind. To begin with, the form of the tools must be noted, together with any characteristics, which appear from the frequency of their occurrence to have been definitely intended by their makers; while at the same time the method of manufacture of the tools must not be lost sight of, for even when making the same kind of tool peoples belonging to different cultures did not always do so in exactly the same way. The importance of this latter consideration has only recently been sufficiently recognised, but

[1] Purely technical considerations, the various methods used for making flint tools, will be dealt with in the next chapter.

it is proving more and more useful to the typologist in his classifications.

As an example of his method of work, let us suppose that an industry obtained by excavating a site has been presented to him for classification. His first business will be to group the artifacts into families, taking some obvious characteristic as a criterion of a family. In practice it is found that the number of these families is small, and indeed in these days they have become perhaps rather stereotyped, and it is only rarely that a new and distinct family is recognised. The characteristics of the various families will be described later on in the chapter dealing with tools. As a result of this preliminary classification, the typologist will find in front of him several heaps of implements, the contents of each heap, from certain points of view, being somewhat similar to each other. Each heap then itself undergoes a second examination, as subdivisions within the families are frequently possible. Consequently each original heap will be found to be divided up into a number of smaller heaps; and sometimes the process can be again repeated, until finally he is left with many small groups each containing almost identical tools.

In the course of this first sorting, the analogy of families has been used; the typologist has as it were separated the Smiths from the Browns, and these again from the Robinsons. But it sometimes happens that the analogy can be still more closely pressed. While all persons called Smith are not interrelated, some of them are, and we can observe more than one generation of Smiths who are immediately connected with one another. The same is sometimes true within the families of tools. We can occasionally note an evolution of a given type from a more primitive to a more evolved form. One

Smith may have children and grandchildren. In this
case the former should clearly be older than the latter
and it is sometimes possible to check the truth of the
hypothesis by stratigraphical means. For example,
there is a kind of tool known as the pointed knife blade
and an evolution from the primitive form (*Audi knife
blade*) to the much more developed *Châtelperron* variety
can be determined on purely typological grounds, and
actually, where a stratigraphical sequence containing
this particular family of tools occurs, the *Audi* variety
is invariably found in layers below those containing
Châtelperron types. Thus the typologist and the stratigrapher can usefully check each other's results, However, such evolutions within the tool-families are all too.
rare and as a rule the various members appear to be
unrelated.

So far we have assumed that the typologist has
been dealing with a single industry only or with industries belonging to one culture. Where, however, he
is concerned with more than one industry belonging to
different cultures he will especially have to keep in mind
the second consideration, i.e. the method of manufacture
of the tools. Often the same family of tools, for example
lance points, will occur in the industries of different
cultures, but frequently not only will the general shape
of the points be somewhat different but the process of
their manufacture, i.e. the way they were chipped, will
vary considerably.

ASSOCIATED FINDS. This line of attack takes into
consideration the objects found in the deposits with
the industries. It is less important than stratigraphy or
typology, being rather useful as a check on the results
obtained by these two than as itself producing much

new information. Nevertheless it is often very helpful when problems of dating are on the *tapis*. To begin with, of course, the investigator must be certain that the association in question is real, i.e. original, and not fortuitous. For instance, surface finds of industries belonging to a certain culture in South Africa are frequently associated with fragments of bottle glass. Now bottle glass was only introduced into that country a comparatively short time ago, therefore, if the association could be proved to be real, the culture in question could not be considered to be of any great antiquity. However, in the case of surface finds it is well-nigh impossible to demonstrate that the association is not accidental, that it is not due to subsequent introduction, in the above case of bottle glass, at a much later date. On the other hand, where an industry occurs sealed in in a layer in a rock-shelter and associated with the bones of an extinct fauna, then the association cannot be considered to be anything but authentic, and the antiquity of the industry must be the same as that of the extinct animals.

But considerations of associated finds are perhaps more specially useful to archaeologists dealing with the somewhat later periods, when interchange of objects by trade or otherwise was more general. Suppose, for example, that an industry of doubtful age has been discovered in one area and associated with it has been found an object, a bead or the like, of peculiar form, which is known from its type to be the work of another people and to be of a definite date. It will then be clear that the industry cannot be assigned to a period earlier in time than the date of the bead; but once again there must be definite evidence that the association is original and not due to subsequent infiltration.

STATE OF PRESERVATION. In discussing the state of preservation of an artifact, the prehistorian must keep two considerations in mind: (i) how much the object has been mechanically rolled or weathered; (ii) how far chemical changes have been at work altering the composition of the specimen.

Mechanical rolling is due, as a rule, to water action and takes place, as its name implies, when an artifact is rolled about in a stream or hurled about on a beach. It tends to produce a rounding of the edges between the various facets, if the implement is of stone or flint, and finally reduces the specimen to a pebble. More fragile materials such as bones, etc., seldom survive much mechanical weathering. As will be at once realised, tools found in rock-shelter homes have seldom undergone this kind of treatment. It is implements found in open stations that have thus suffered.

It is clearly not at all true to say that a mechanically rolled specimen must be necessarily older than one that has not so suffered. A tool may have been dropped by man at some very early date and become almost immediately incorporated in a brick-earth or gravel and there remained unmoved until excavated by the prehistorian. At a much later date another tool dropped on the same place may, owing to some natural chance, have been carried away and rolled about in a stream for a considerable time before it, in its turn, came to rest and became incorporated in some deposit. Obviously in this case the more worn specimen will not actually be so old as the unrolled one. All that can be definitely stated from a study of mechanical rolling alone is whether a specimen has or has not been moved far from the place where it was dropped. When a specimen has had to travel a long way it is seldom that it escapes damage. Where it has become incorporated in some deposit close to where it was dropped, as a rule it is found to be but little rolled.

It sometimes happens that when an industry is examined by the typologist, he finds tools, which on purely typological grounds he would consider to be of a certain age, associated with others which for similar reasons would be classed as more recent. In such cases it will often be found that the older tools show a greater degree of mechanical rolling than do those of the later date, a confirmation of the conclusion arrived at typologically and perhaps open to some such explanation as the following. It not infrequently happens that a river denudes away a gravel bed and redeposits it elsewhere. In such cases of course any implements contained in that bed will also suffer denudation and redeposition, in which case they will, as a rule, show a greater rolling than do the tools of subsequent date that were dropped by man near by and incorporated in the new gravel as it was forming.[1] This is only one example of the use of a study of mechanical rolling to the prehistorian and it indicates that while it is dangerous to deduce any very definite information from such a study by itself, it can be very useful when employed in conjunction with one of the other methods of approach to the problem. Once again, as with the question of associated finds, it is useful rather as a check than as itself a direct source of information.

Coming now to the second consideration of how chemical changes may have been at work in altering the composition of the specimen, this will be found to be chiefly important in the case of flint, where chemical

---

[1] The age of a gravel, then, must usually be that of the culture represented by the contained unrolled specimens.

changes at the surface produce a definite skin or patina. This matter will be more particularly considered in a subsequent chapter (p. 54). It suffices here to say that chemical weathering of flint is also very capricious, and will not infrequently be found to be different on two sides of the same implement. Within a restricted area, such as a single gravel pit, however, it can be of considerable importance.

Tools made of bone or antler, etc., undergo a special kind of chemical weathering. When fresh they contain a good deal of organic matter: soup can be made by boiling them in water. But in the course of time this disappears and only the mineral substance remains. Bones in this condition are naturally very fragile, but frequently the organic matter is replaced by a deposit of mineral material. The bones are then described as being fossilised, the cellular structure still surviving and being visible to the naked eye. Sometimes matters go a stage farther, the whole bone is replaced by stone, merely the general shape surviving; it is then described as being mineralised. The words *fossilised* and *mineralised* are used somewhat loosely, there is, however, a gradation between them. Once again no information as to age can be deduced from the study of fossilisation of the bone tools alone. The surrounding conditions are the controlling factors and bones may even sometimes survive for a very long time while still containing much of their organic contents; on the other hand complete fossilisation or even mineralisation may under certain circumstances be very rapid.

SCIENTIFIC METHODS FOR DATING FINDS. Of recent years much valuable help, especially as regards dating, has been supplied by other scientific disciplines.

Thus the physicist by the radioactive carbon (C^{14}) method can in some cases determine the actual age in time of a given specimen, while the chemist by the determination of the fluorine content in the bones found at a given site can say whether they are all of the same age or not. The nitrogen and phosphate contents of the soils also can sometimes give important information, while the palaeobotanist can determine the climates, and so often the relative ages, of many of the later cultures by the method of pollen analysis. Finally the petrologist, too, has been roped in to find out whence came the raw materials used in tool making, especially in cases when some fine-grained rock other than flint is in question. When it can be stated with certainty where the raw material occurs it is often possible to suggest primitive "trade routes" and other lines of contact between different cultures. Of these new aids to study perhaps the three more important ones are the C^{14} method of dating, the fluorine test and pollen analysis. A very brief account of each will, therefore, be given.

Cosmic rays which are continually bombarding the earth produce in the atmosphere neutrons which in turn hit the atoms of nitrogen in the air and are absorbed by their nuclei. But these nuclei are unstable and each throws off a proton with its positive electric charge, leaving what should be the atom of nitrogen (atomic weight 14) with the residual negative electric charge. But this becomes a carbon atom of atomic weight 14 instead of 12 as is usual for carbon. C^{14} behaves like C^{12} and combines with oxygen to form carbon dioxide which is absorbed by plant life in the normal way, and through plant life by animals. But C^{14} atoms disintegrate. As long as cosmic rays bombard the earth a norm is reached in the atmosphere, and therefore too in plant and animal life which is continually absorbing the $C^{14}O_2$. But when a plant or animal dies absorption ceases and disintegration takes place. In something over 5600 years only half of the C^{14} remains and in another similar period only half of that residue. If, therefore, the amount of C^{14} still present in the charcoal or bones found in a given level can be determined the actual age can with reasonable accuracy be deduced. This newly discovered method of dating is of the greatest importance and where proof from other sources has been available has been amazingly accurate. But there are many practical dangers to guard against. Specimens for analysis must be collected with meticulous care to avoid admixture with the specimen either of extraneous live material, whereby the readings would naturally be too high, or vice versa. Again the human factor in the actual determination has to be remembered. Results are most accurate for medium dates and beyond 30,000 years become less reliable.

The fluorine test depends on the fact that bone (calcium phosphate) absorbs fluorine dissolved in per-colating water, resulting finally in the formation of a stable fluor-apatite. At any given site, then, where bones, whether animal or human, occur, should they all be of the same age they will all yield the same per-centage of fluor-apatite. But let us suppose that at a given site there are a number of bones of domestic animals as well as a human skull. If the human skull yields a far greater percentage of fluor-apatite than do the other bones it will be older than they are. If the percentage is similar then the human skull is contem-porary with the domestic animals. Once again there are dangers to guard against when using this method of comparative dating. The rate of absorption depends on the amount of fluorine in the percolating water. If this is large there may be a great deal of fluor-apatite present even in the case of fairly modern bones and the difference between the percentages in the bones of different ages may be less marked in consequence. The fluorine test has been useful at such sites as Galley Hill on the Lower Thames where the skull was shown to be not very ancient.

The tree composition of a forest depends partly on the soil and largely on the climate. Should forests occur on the borders of a fen the pollen from the trees gets blown over the fen and becomes incorporated and preserved in the accumulating peat. Should the climate change, new kinds of trees will replace the old, and different kinds of pollen, for each tree has its own recognisable shape of pollen grain, will be swallowed in the peat, by now, of course at a higher level. A section through the accumulated peats will therefore yield a series of layers containing pollen grains from the trees which formed the forests—grains whose presence can not only be recognised but their numbers counted and proportions determined and any climatic changes thereby assessed. Should man have lived in the vicinity it sometimes happens that his tools, too, get into the various peat layers. Thus becomes possible a correlation between the various cultures present and the climate changes that have taken place. This method of study is more particularly important in early holocene times, in the case of mesolithic cultures. Of course the method is not fool-proof. Latitude, longitude and altitude have to be taken into account. In the north the forest composition may be still a pine-hazel complex while to the south at the same time the same culture will be found associated with a mixed oak forest. But it has been of great archaeological importance and help of recent years.

Chapter III

TOOL-MAKING

UNTIL upper palaeolithic times man fashioned his tools almost exclusively of stone, but with the coming of the Aurignacians (*Homo sapiens*) other materials were added, viz. bone, horn, antler and ivory. No doubt throughout palaeolithic times wood must have been employed for many purposes but naturally this material has not survived. At the same time the student must always beware of judging the importance of a prehistoric culture solely by the quality of the stone industries which are found. He should always remember that a comparatively poor stone industry may have been accompanied by a richer one made from perishable materials.

STONE TOOLS

For making his tools palaeolithic man employed any kind of suitable stone which was available, and, where they happened to occur in the locality, fine-grained rocks were often employed. But however fine-grained such rocks may be, they cannot be readily fashioned by knapping and the resultant tool has an edge which though tough can seldom be made even or sharp. The reason for this is of course clear. A rock is not a homogeneous substance; it is composed of a number of minerals and these vary in hardness and may or may not cleave readily in all directions. It follows that, even when fine-grained, any attempt to produce a cutting edge by chipping would be bound to be somewhat of a failure, and it is indeed marvellous what comparatively excellent results were sometimes obtained even when quite refractory material was used.

But there is one substance which is very suitable for the purpose, being so homogeneous as almost to act as if it were a mineral and cleaving readily in any direction, namely flint. In composition flint is a hydrated silica, having a variable amount of water loosely held in combination. It is of common occurrence in nature, appearing frequently as bands of nodules in chalk deposits. When for any reason the chalk matrix gets denuded away, the harder flint nodules remain on the surface of the ground, and such is the origin of the vast spreads of flint that occur in many parts of East Anglia. The exact mode of formation of flint has been a matter of some controversy, but it is fortunately not of very great importance to the prehistorian who, after all, is only concerned with the substance once it has got into the hands of man. In many cases, however, we must look to organic action for the explanation. A number of fossil sponges required silica to build up their internal structure, and had the power of abstracting the necessary material from sea water which carries it in solution in small quantities. Flint nuclei were thus formed which grew bigger by a process of accretion. It would seem, however, that though this is what frequently happened it is not the only possible way of accounting for its formation.

FRACTURE OF FLINT BY PERCUSSION. Flint is a very brittle substance, and it fractures in a rather peculiar way. Suppose a lump of flint be taken and a hard blow dealt it, the force of the blow being concentrated as far as possible at one point and directed towards the middle of the lump, in nine cases out of ten the result will in actual practice merely be a general shattering of the whole substance, but in the tenth case the lump will break up into two parts in such a way that the one piece, a sort of cap with a peculiar shaped hollow on its under surface, can be lifted off the other piece which has a corresponding nipple-shaped protuberance exactly fitting the hollow. This protuberance is found to consist of a double cone, that is, of a cone with steep sides truncated and surmounted by another whose sides are inclined at a far smaller angle to the horizontal, there being a regular shoulder where the two meet. Around both cones can be seen rings. The projection is known as the cone, or perhaps more strictly speaking, cones of percussion, and the corresponding hollow in the cap which comes off as the negative cone. Reference to Fig. 1 will make clearer what is meant by this description. It must be remembered that the whole phenomenon is the result of a single blow.

Suppose, however, that instead of striking our lump of flint towards its middle the blow be applied at one edge. In this case a flake will be struck off and when the two pieces are studied it will be found that the flake (or very occasionally the main piece, i.e. the core) carries on its surface a swelling near the point of impact of the blow. This is known as the bulb of percussion (Fig. 1, 3). On the core from which the flake has been struck, there is naturally a hollow corresponding to the bulb, known as the negative bulb of percussion. In a sense the bulb can be considered as a portion of a cone of percussion. The point of impact of the blow at the apex of the bulb is often visible and the rings we saw as complete circles round the cone now take the form of arcs of circles

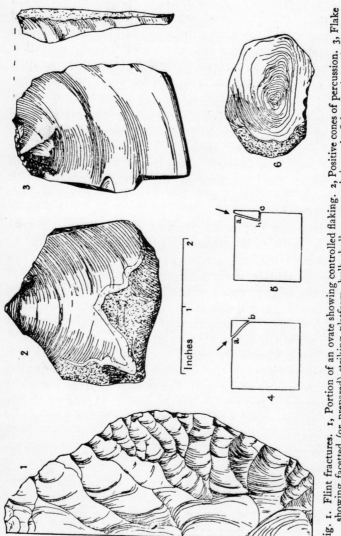

Fig. 1. Flint fractures. 1, Portion of an ovate showing controlled flaking. 2, Positive cones of percussion. 3, Flake showing facetted (or prepared) striking platform, bulb, bulbar scar and rings; the flake terminates in a hinge fracture. 4, 5, Diagrams illustrating feather edge and step flaking. 6, A piece of flint showing thermal fracture rings.

surrounding the point of impact. It should be noted that these rings, surrounding as they do the point of impact of the blow, are themselves indicative of the direction from which the blow in question has been struck. Wherever we find such rings on a flake or flake scar, we can always be certain that the blow which caused them must have been delivered into the concavities of the rings. It follows then that where we have to deal with an implement flaked all over by man, even when subsequent trimming has removed most of the bulbs we can—from a study of the rings—still determine the direction of the several blows which removed the flakes and left the flake scars we are scrutinising.

It is really not a bad practice for a student to take such a tool as a coup-de-poing (see p. 60 and Fig. 2) and mark with little arrows in ordinary ink (which can be subsequently washed off) the directions from which came the blows responsible for the various flake scars. As a result he will obtain interesting information as to the method of manufacture of the tool and the way it was held when being fashioned.

When a flake is knocked off by a very hard blow it sometimes happens that shatter lines are seen radiating from the point of impact. These shatter lines naturally form radii of the rings already described; they indicate lines of weakness and show that the blow which had been given was too strenuous. When a well-formed bulb of percussion, such as frequently occurs on Mousterian flakes, etc., is studied, a small flake facet (Fig. 1, 3) will frequently be noticed on the bulb; this is known as the bulbar scar (French=*éraillure*). It is not due to a subsequent attempt by prehistoric man to remove the bulbar swelling by further chipping, but seems to be

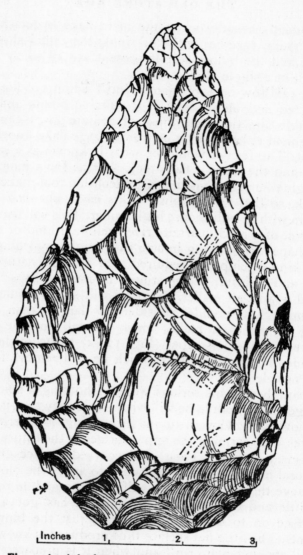

Inches   1   2   3

Fig. 2. An Acheulean coup-de-poing from Hoxne, Suffolk.

produced naturally when the main flake is detached. The bulb, together with the rings, the radial shatter lines and the bulbar scar if present are all solely the result of a single blow.

It can now be appreciated that if a lump of flint is selected and blows dealt it at suitable points and in suitable directions, an object of definite shape can be fashioned either from it or from a large flake knocked off it. The former would be what is known as a core-tool and the latter a flake-tool. Let us for a moment imagine ourselves visiting a palaeolithic tool-maker at work, so that we can observe his *modus operandi*. To begin with he will choose his hammer. This will usually consist of a hard quartzite river pebble, round or oval in shape, and varying in size and weight according as the kind of chipping required is of a rough nature or fine and delicate; or sometimes, he may perhaps have used a wooden mallet. Next he will select a suitable natural flint nodule considerably larger than the tool he wishes to make, which we will imagine is a Mousterian side-scraper (Fig. 12, 2) to be made on a suitably prepared flake which he will remove from the nodule.

Now begins his serious work. Choosing a suitable bulge on the nodule he will where necessary trim it and remove any awkward lumps by striking off a series of flakes, thus forming the upper surface of the future tool (primary flaking). Then if the curved surface of the natural nodule makes it awkward to apply the blow to remove the main flake, he will turn the nodule round a little and chip away again until he has got a flat surface on to which he can strike just the blow he wants. The little flat surface thus produced is known as the "striking platform" and when it is prepared artificially, as has just been described, is called a "facetted" or "prepared" striking platform (Fig. 1, 3). This preparation being accomplished he strikes the main blow on to his platform and removes the flake. He has now no more to do but to give his flake its final trimming to make the sharp convex working edge which it should have. Taking a smaller hammer stone and holding the flake horizontally, he produces this by chipping away all down one side a number of little flakes whose scars intersect with the main flake surface (trimming or secondary flaking). It should be noticed in passing that the direction of the blows which made the facetted striking platform was at right angles to that which knocked off the main flake, and again the direction of the blows which made the working edge was more or less at right angles both to that which made the main flake surface and to those which formed the prepared striking platform.

But it is not sufficient merely to say that our craftsman "knocked off" flakes; we must examine in greater detail how he performed this action. If a piece of flint is taken and a blow struck on its edge, a different result will be obtained according as the blow is struck (i) outwards, away from the centre of the flint, or (ii) inwards, towards the thickness of its substance (Fig. 1, 4 and 5). A blow represents a certain amount of force which passes rapidly through air, but when entering the denser medium of the flint, very soon grows less and less in much the same way as an individual running freely in the open countryside is brought almost to a standstill when he tries to get through a dense crowd. In the case of the first kind of blow, although this force is considerably lessened when passing into the flint, it has not so very far to go, and so gets through the dense medium out into the air again before being completely dissipated. As a result a clean flake[1] is removed and a smooth flake scar left. In passing an exploratory finger from any one such flake scar to a similar neighbour no impeding ridge will be encountered, a finger-nail placed at *a* (Fig. 1, *4*) will slide over the angles at *a* and *b* smoothly and without meeting any obstruction.

In the second case, on the other hand, the direction of the blow is inwards into the substance of the flint and its force is spent before getting through to the other side. There results a fracture or crack in the flint, starting at the point of impact of the blow, but coming to an end after the flint has only been partially penetrated. In some cases nothing further happens and the little cracks can sometimes be seen, but since they represent lines of weakness subsequent weathering frequently makes them more visible. But as a rule the blow, besides forming the crack, also has a shattering effect and a small portion of the flint gets broken off, roughly at right angles to the line of the crack, and a flake scar results. But what a different flake scar! There is found as it were a sort of step (Fig. 1, *5*, *a b c*) and it is no longer possible for the finger to pass smoothly from one chip to the next. The step effectively prevents such transit. In the first case the trimming is said to be of the "feather edge" variety, the result of "free flaking," and in the second case of the "step" or "resolved" kind. While it is untrue to affirm that either of these methods of flaking

---

[1] HINGE FRACTURE. Occasionally a flake may be observed whose edge will be found to curl over at the end farthest from the bulb. This phenomenon is known as hinge fracture (Fig. 1, *3*). Prehistoric man could not make use of it as it cannot be produced at will. It is therefore of little importance to the prehistorian though he should be able to recognise it.

was exclusively used at any one time or by people of any one culture, it can be safely stated that step flaking was very commonly used for secondary working in middle palaeolithic times. In the nature of the case scars resulting from step flaking are, on the whole, rather smaller than those produced by free flaking. This technique is, therefore, chiefly employed for secondary working, and is particularly used for sharpening the working edges of the tools. Such flake scars usually show the bulbar rings very clearly. In the case of free flaking, where the blow goes slick through the flint like a knife through an apple, although these rings occur they are usually fewer, flatter and less well marked.

It will now be clear in what manner the difference between these two methods of flaking depends on the direction in which the blows are struck, and that this difference represents to some extent a real choice in the technique of manufacture. Free flaking very often removes roughly quadrangular flakes, leaving corresponding flake scars on the core but, sometimes, on such tools as coups-de-poing flake scars can be noted which are much more regular in shape, being long and narrow and shallow with roughly parallel sides, so that the flakes which have been removed must have been quite thin compared with their length, much thinner than is usually the case when free flaking is employed (Fig. 1, 1). Rings are prominently seen, being often numerous and close together. These phenomena are the result of what has been called "controlled" flaking, and it has been claimed that they result from the use of wooden mallets instead of hammerstones, the soft wood producing something of pressure action instead of the sharp percussion of the harder stone hammer. It has also been suggested that the *modus operandi* for producing such flaking consisted in so holding the flint to be flaked in the flat of the hand that the blows could be struck near the finger tips and directed along the line of the fingers, whose pressure on the flint would tend to damp down the impetus of the blow in their direction, thus partially changing its character by turning as it were percussion into pressure. For, as will be seen from studying a subsequent paragraph, many of the phenomena observable in the case of this controlled flaking are simply those found on objects fractured by pressure.

An ingenious method of flint tool-making was practised at a very early date by the peoples of certain cultures. Before the discovery of pressure flaking (with which we shall deal later) it was by no means always easy for the craftsman to obtain a large tool, such as a disc with sharp edges, which would be very thin compared with its size. In order to do this by percussion alone, the following method was adopted. A suitable nodule of flint was chosen and a selected upper surface worked over by flaking until a flattish face resulted. The sides of the nodule were now boldly trimmed away so that the future tool was as it were blocked out, though still attached to the core. A striking platform was next prepared and a single blow then detached the required tool which would consist of an object whose upper surface was flat as a result of the primary flaking while still on the nodule, and whose under surface was a flake surface resulting from the blow of detachment. In the case of large specimens any shatter effect which might result from striking off the implement from the core might have been nullified by burying the core in sand before detaching the tool, or by binding a skin round it. This method of tool making is known as the Levallois flake technique; the detached tools being called by this name and the cores from which they were struck, tortoise cores. The name Levallois flake is derived from a suburb of Paris where certain flakes made in this manner were first recognised. As these happened to be oval, the cores from which they were struck necessarily somewhat resembled a tortoise in shape, hence the core name (Fig. 6, 2 and 4).

Another way of breaking flint or rock is by the so-called swinging-blow method. This is particularly useful where large blocks of material have to be broken up. The lump of material is taken up in the hands and with a swinging blow hit against a hard block of rock or anvil. As a result a flake is detached with a single-facetted striking platform inclined at a high angle, about 120°, to the main flake surface. While this method of fracturing flint was in common use among the so-called Clacton cultures it must be remembered that the swinging-blow technique was used at all times and in all areas, more especially where flakes had to be removed from large nuclei. As it occurs so frequently in the case of Clacton industries the resulting flake is often called a Clacton flake and the swinging-blow method the Clacton technique. But the student must beware of muddling up a technique with a culture. The so-called Clacton technique was not confined to the people of the true Clacton culture.

Certain industries in upper palaeolithic times present us with a type of flaking known as "fluting". Here long, narrow, shallow flakes with parallel sides have been removed, and the resulting tool is often of extreme beauty (Fig. 15, 4). As its name implies, this type of flaking can be fancifully compared with the shallow flutings such as are sometimes seen on architectural columns; but how prehistoric man managed to strike off these thin, narrow flakes is not clearly understood.

A long, narrow flake with more or less parallel sides, and often thin and flat--relative to its length is called a blade (Fig. 6, 3). Such blades must usually have been detached by means of a punch as the point of impact must be small and the direction of the blow accurate. A bone punch would serve the purpose. It is significant that blade industries appear with the upper palaeolithic when bone was in frequent use. Of course the term blade industry does not imply that every tool must be made on a blade. But the proportion of blade tools to those made on flakes or cores is high.

Nature, unaided, frequently fractures flint by percussion, and most of the phenomena which we have been describing, with the exception, perhaps, of that due to controlled flaking, can be observed on specimens fractured solely by natural means. Imagine a piece of flint rolling down the hillside in a mountain torrent. It is hurled about from side to side and knocked against the rocks in its descent, receiving blows from all directions and becoming covered with flake scars. This statement is perhaps not always literally true. It is often rather that the flint itself gets turned about in the stream and so when the rings of each flake scar are studied the blows have apparently come from all directions. For convenience, however, it is usual to imagine either that all the blows come from one direction only and the flint is twisted about, or that the flint is held constant and the blows come from different directions. Naturally in the case of our stream both factors come into play, although the general downhill movement tends to make the direction of the blows more or less constant. From the point of view of the argument it matters not at all, but for descriptive purposes it is easier to imagine that one factor is always constant. Let us imagine another case where a piece of flint has become wedged between two rocks at the bottom of a stream, and receives blows from other stones that are being tumbled along by the water. Here, as the stream is necessarily flowing downhill, the direction of the blows given to the piece of flint will always be the same, or nearly so. The same sort of phenomena can be observed on the sea beach. A pebble hurled about freely by the force of the waves will be chipped in all directions, but one wedged on the shore will show only a single direction of battering blows—incidentally rather due to the sucking back of the stones against the flint than to any hurling of pebbles against it by the force of the waves. It follows, then, that nature can chip a flint by blows coming from every direction, or from one direction.

The one thing nature cannot do is to chip a flint in one direction, then turn it at right angles and repeat the process, and then again turn it more or less at right angles and trim an edge: this process involves the control of the human will. If a student will look back a few paragraphs to the imaginary picture of the prehistoric tool-maker fashioning a Mousterian side-scraper, he will note such distinctive directions of blows occurring. We thus have a criterion to enable us to state with absolute certainty whether a chipped flint is an artifact or not. If there are two, or much better three, definite directions from which came the blows responsible for the flake scars, then the specimen has been humanly fashioned. Of course when studying an industry it is not always necessary to demonstrate this proof in every case. Man was perfectly capable of choosing a flat piece of natural flint of suitable shape and size and turning it into an effective tool by giving it a sharp working edge, when the blows will have come from one direction only. When we have to deal with an undoubted occupation level where artifacts abound, whether in a rock-shelter site or open station, there is often every reason to accept as artifacts specimens which theoretically could have been made by natural means alone. But in other instances where important results depend on the acceptance or rejection as artifacts of certain chipped specimens, it is necessary to invoke this criterion, and to demonstrate by its means the certain necessary presence of human beings who must have designed and fashioned the objects.[1]

Frequently beautiful specimens are collected showing but a single trimmed edge made by blows from only one direction. In most cases, as has been said above, it is impossible to be sure that these are really artifacts, but it is true to say that nature is somewhat rough and irregular in her trimming, especially when she is using the percussion method, and, where a percussed trimmed edge has regular little flake scars carefully truncating the edges between two other larger scars, it is likely that man had a hand in the fashioning. Nature is all too frequently inclined to batter, and this battering effect is a very recognisable and tell-tale sign that the chipping on the object has been purely her doing. Unfortunately, no amount of description even in detail can be as helpful to the student in this matter as can a small collection of natural and artificial fractures set out for his study, and it is therefore to be hoped that our museums, both great and small, will not neglect to make such exhibitions a permanent feature of their

[1] Only true artifacts show evidence of real design in the knapping.

work. It is just as important to set out for public use a case of carefully selected and well-labelled natural fractures as it is to exhibit an endless series of tools, often of quite similar type, that may happen to occur abundantly in the locality.

PRESSURE FLAKING. Percussion flaking has been dealt with in detail, as it is perhaps the most important method of fracturing flint used by palaeolithic man; but pressure flaking, it must not be forgotten, was not only very much in use at one period (the Solutrean, see Fig. 7, 2, 6 and 8) but was also probably much employed throughout upper palaeolithic times for finer secondary working. Pressure flaking, as its name implies, consists in the removal of small flakes by the application of pressure at a given point on a flint edge with a suitable implement made of stone or bone. Usually only fairly small thin flakes of flint can be removed, for the pressure that can be applied is seldom sufficient to remove thick flakes. A characteristic appearance of the resulting flake surface is frequently such as to give rise to the term "fish-scale" flaking. Such flaking is often observable on many of our early metal age flint tools in East Anglia. Indeed, it is almost a criterion that can be used to separate these metal age artifacts from those of earlier neolithic date. Next we can notice the pronounced and close-packed bulbar rings on each of the flake scars. Where a specimen has not been subsequently weathered, these close-packed rings reflect and refract the light in such a way as to give it a glassy or waxy appearance. While bulbs of pressure, corresponding to bulbs of percussion, occur, these are far less pronounced than when percussion has been employed. As has been said, pressure flaking is especially suitable for fine workmanship, since the craftsman is able to apply pressure at exactly the point he desires and to exactly the degree that is required. The connection between it and controlled flaking has already been mentioned. Controlled flaking represents, as it were, a sort of transition between the two methods of fracturing flint.

Nature, of course, can also fracture flint by pressure. The weight of a vast mass of superincumbent earth on a bed containing flints closely packed together will often produce pressure fractures. Again, a gravel terrace running along the edge of a steep hillside and containing a number of flints in contact with one another, will sometimes tend to "creep" somewhat downhill towards the bottom of the valley under the influence of gravity. Slight differential movements within the gravel terrace set up pressures among the various flints, and fractures result. There is no need to suggest further possibilities, the student can imagine them for himself. It only remains to say that pressure-flaked objects in which the force came from one direction or from many directions and was due solely to natural means are also of common occurrence; but, as in the case of percussion, nature cannot by pressure flake specimens, the pressure having come from two, or better still three, specific directions only. Only man can design.

THERMAL ACTION. Flint expands slightly on being heated and contracts again when cooled; it is, however, a very bad conductor of heat, and the interior of a block of flint cannot therefore readily adapt itself to the results of rapid changes of temperature which affect the surface, and fractures consequently appear. This method of flaking flint thermally does not seem to have been employed by palaeolithic man. But natural specimens of

PLATE II

View of the cave-mouth at Castillo with the village of Puente Viesgo in the valley below.

it are so common and characteristic, and objects obviously thus fractured are so often collected by the amateur who frequently considers them to be artifacts, that a word or two about the phenomena connected with it will not be out of place.

A flat surface of flint resulting from a thermal fracture shows a series of irregular closed rings about a central point, which is either a small depression or a tiny pimple (Fig. 1, 6). Even when a specimen has subsequently been broken in half and the rings therefore are no longer closed, their irregularity distinguishes them at once from bulbar rings whether the result of percussion or of pressure. Again, a thermally fractured surface has a characteristic appearance which unfortunately cannot be described, but which once seen is seldom afterwards mistaken. Frost action frequently causes a pocking of the surface, small discs of flint coming off. These are sometimes of considerable size, and have been mistaken when subsequently weathered for the opercula of certain fossil shell fish.

A special variety of fracture known as "starch" fracture is responsible for bars of flint whose sides are apparently formed of long parallel facets, the whole frequently having a sort of columnar structure. That the facets forming the column of flint are not the result of percussion or pressure flaking can be clearly perceived from the complete absence of bulbs or rings. Although on a very small scale, these bars of flint due to starch fracture may be compared with the basalt columns of the Giants' Causeway. It would seem that this kind of fracture is the result of breakage due to shrinkage of the flint. Starch fractured specimens are fairly common on the surface of the land in East Anglia, and again and again they have been mistaken for cores from which prehistoric man had struck off long flakes for tool-making purposes.

WEATHERING OF FLINT: PATINA. The effects of the weathering of stone implements resulting from rolling and other mechanical means, and their importance to the prehistorian, have already been considered in a previous chapter, and we have just dealt with thermal and starch fractures. It will be convenient, therefore, now to consider the results of chemical weathering which frequently take place at the surface of flint. As has been said, flint is composed of silica containing in loose combination a variable quantity of water, and it would seem that, under certain circumstances, some of this water can be given off, leaving a sort of skin of silica on the outer surface of the flint. The process is, in all probability, far more complicated than this simple statement suggests, but the subject has been little investigated and its exact chemistry is not really properly understood.

The skin of chemically weathered flint is known as the patina. It varies in thickness from a small fraction of a millimetre to several millimetres. When very thick and subsequently weathered, often showing a rough nubbly appearance, it is called cortex, and obviously cortex and patina are in many cases closely connected. A thin skin of patina is at first white but, unlike flint itself, it is to some extent porous, and as flints, whether natural pebbles or artifacts, are often embedded in gravels containing iron salts, the patina frequently absorbs some of the iron products and becomes coloured an ochreous yellow or orange.[1] But in this connection

[1] A certain characteristic kind of patchy ochreous patina is, for obvious reasons, known as "toad-belly patina".

the student must take considerable care. Natural flint in its pure state is colourless; almost invariably, however, it contains small quantities of various impurities that give it a strong colouration. Thus the East Anglian flint contains a small quantity of carbonaceous matter and is generally black. Other flint is grey. Again, certain flint deposits in northern France are honey coloured, others toffee coloured. Trouble must be taken to distinguish between the colouration of the unpatinated flint and that due to the subsequent colouration of the patinated surface. Furthermore—an added complication—a natural black flint, slightly patinated on its surface, will have a blue appearance due to the black colour showing through the thin white skin of patina. In common parlance this is described as a blue patina, but actually the coloured appearance is thus due to a totally different cause from that of a normal ochreous specimen, where the colour is caused by a subsequent staining of the white patina itself. Normally, patinated flints, especially when the patina is deep, have a matt surface; but where any rolling—more especially where the deposit in which the flint occurs is of a soft nature such as a loam or brick-earth—has taken place this matt surface becomes glossy.

It must be borne in mind that the formation of patina is very capricious and results from conditions as yet imperfectly understood. The patina on specimens in different parts of a single gravel pit may vary and often, when a large flat artifact has been lying horizontally in a deposit, the upper surface will be found to have a different patina from the under one. Contact with lime seems to affect matters, and specimens found buried in chalk, even when of very considerable age, frequently appear to be unpatinated, while others, more modern, but found elsewhere, show a considerable degree of patination. The prehistorian should, therefore, draw conclusions from patination with discrimination. No great antiquity can be postulated for a specimen simply because it is deeply patinated. On the other hand, should it be found on typological grounds that two distinct industries are apparently present in a given bed, this conclusion can be reinforced if it is found that the one series shows a different patination from the other. Again, when examining a gravel face in a pit, if it is found that the natural pebbles and artifacts from one layer show a different patination, either in degree or in kind, from those found in another layer, there is good hope that, when the workmen's dumps which come from both layers are examined, the artifacts, found in these "concentrates", can be correctly assigned to their beds of origin.

Sometimes when the surface of a flint has been scratched as a result of ice action, the scratches "weather out" and become patinated white, and thus the surface of the flint becomes covered with irregularly crossing white lines. This very characteristic phenomenon is known as "basket work patina".

DESCRIPTION OF STONE TOOLS. It often becomes necessary for the student to describe a tool briefly and succinctly. For this purpose some descriptive scheme must be employed. While it is not suggested that the following plan is by any means the only one to follow, or even necessarily the best, at the same time, until the student has evolved a clear logical system of his own, it can be employed by him with advantage.

To begin with, the material from which the tool is made should be named, whether it is flint, chalcedony or chert (the latter being an impure variety of flint), quartz, or a rock such as quartzite or diorite, etc., or some natural glass such as obsidian. The natural colouration of the material should then be carefully noted, and for this purpose it is well to find some small modern fracture which has penetrated through the outer skin or patina and exposed the inner material—it is rare to come across a specimen which has not been slightly damaged sufficiently to give this information.

Secondly, the state of preservation should be considered and described: is the object much, slightly or not at all rolled? Do the edges between the facets show any rounding or battering, or are they still sharp and fresh? The patina also must be described. Is it uniform all over the surface of the tool or patchy? Is it thick or thin? Here again our small modern fracture will help us. What is the colour of the patina, and does it present a matt or glossy appearance?

Thirdly, the primary flaking must be described. This blocks out the tool and is therefore concerned with the general shape of the object which must be described. Is it flaked all over on both sides, or is one surface a main flake surface? If the latter, are a bulb, bulbar scar and rings present, and is there a prepared striking platform or not?[1] The flake scars themselves, are they due to free, resolved, or controlled flaking?

Fourthly, the secondary working must be considered. Whereas the shape of the tool in all directions has just been dealt with, the working edge or edges must now be described. How are they formed and what type of flaking is used for the purpose, is it a case of feather edge, resolved or pressure flaking, or of fluting?

Fifthly, any special notes should be made, particularly

[1] If so, at roughly what angle is it inclined to the main flake surface?

of any outstanding feature that can help the student in making up his mind as to the next and last heading.

Sixthly, the name and age of the tool should be given.

All this sounds long and complicated. Actually after a little practice it is seldom that more than a few minutes are required for the complete description of even a complicated tool. Naturally it has been necessary to evolve a scheme that will enable the most complicated implements to be described. When dealing with simpler types, omissions can obviously easily be made, but taken as a whole it does enable a proper description of a flint implement to be made which can be interpreted by and is therefore of some use to fellow students elsewhere.

MATERIALS OTHER THAN STONE OR FLINT

Materials such as bone, horn, antler and ivory were very rarely used for tool making in stone age industries before upper palaeolithic times; but in the Magdalenian period especially they were frequently so employed, and very beautifully made implements were fashioned from them. At first a small portion of bone was selected and this was ground down, probably in a bit of grooved sandstone, until the required shape was attained. In the nature of the case, however, only certain kinds of bone tools could be made, as the hollow interior of bones presented difficulties. It was all right when a large round polisher was required, but, unless a fragment was used or the bone happened to be that of a very small animal, there was a danger, when making small tools, of removing most of the outer bony substance in the process of manufacture. In Magdalenian times, when small tools such as needles were required, a new method was evolved. A large bone was selected and along it were carved with a flint tool two deep longitudinal grooves. The solid plate of bone lying between these two roughly parallel grooves was then removed by a blow, and tools were fashioned from it.

There is little further to add in connection with these materials that does not result from a study of the tools themselves and these will be considered in the next chapter.

Chapter IV

TOOL FAMILIES

[In this chapter the student will find a brief account of the chief families of tools. It is intended rather as a reference chapter than as one to be read straight through. The tool families are given alphabetically.]

STONE TOOLS

AWLS (Fig. 5, 6, 7 and 8). Any suitably pointed piece of stone or flint will serve as an awl. But in a prepared specimen the working end either shows careful trimming all round (true awl) or, when the awl is made on a flake or blade, the trimming is sometimes only carried round through 180°, the flat flake surface being left untrimmed (pseudo-awl). In the former case, of course, a section through the point would be roughly circular, and in the second case D-shaped. Awls vary in size; minute specimens such as were used for piercing the eyes of bone needles have frequently been found, while others are large and coarse. In France these latter are sometimes called *tarauds*.

COUPS-DE-POING (Figs. 2 and 3). As the evolution of the coup-de-poing tool family is intimately connected with the development of the Chelleo-Acheulean culture, a full description of its various members will be given when that culture and its characteristic features are described. It will be enough to say here that essentially coups-de-poing are core-tools (p. 42) having both their upper and lower faces trimmed all over and a sharp edge between them except, generally, round the butt end. Two main varieties of the tool can be recognised, the one pear-shaped and pointed, the other flatter and

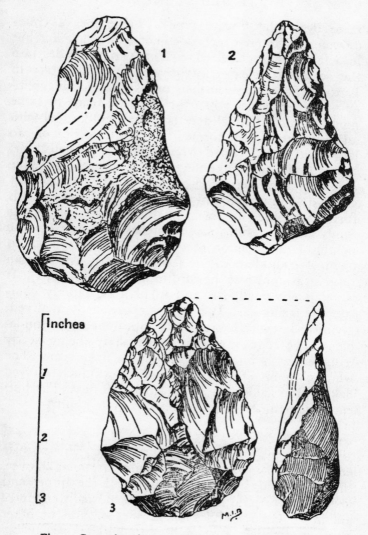

Fig. 3. Coups-de-poing. 1, Chellean. 2, Late Acheulean.
3, Ovate showing Z-twist.

more oval—the "ovate type". Sometimes a coup-
de-poing is found which does not end in a point but
in a fairly wide chisel edge. This variety grades into
the so-called "cleaver" type which, though rare in
Europe, is common elsewhere in lower palaeolithic coup-
de-poing industries when the tools are made of some
non-flint rock. The cleaver is a flat axe-like tool with
a broad cutting edge formed by the intersection of two
large flake scars inclined to one another at a small angle.
A brittle substance like flint is quite unsuitable for the
manufacture of this kind of implement. Occasionally
coups-de-poing are found which have their pointed ends
further trimmed to form small awls, and almost as
rarely with carefully made notches not far from the
points of the tools on one side. A rather specialised
form of coup-de-poing is found in early Mousterian
times, it is known as the cordiform type (Fig. 12, *1*). It
is relatively small, flat and in plan is roughly equi-
laterally triangular. The base is occasionally incurved,
giving a somewhat heart-shaped appearance to the implement. The edges are straight and sharp, being neatly
trimmed with fine, small, resolved, flake scars. The
whole chipping of the tool, indeed, shows much resolved
flaking, the flake scars being small and neat. The butt
end is sometimes sharp, sometimes quite blunt.

DISCS AND CHOPPERS (Fig. 5, *10*). These implements
are round, oval or roughly square with very irregular
edges. They consist of pieces of flint trimmed all over,
the intersections of the trimmings of the upper and
lower faces forming the sharp edges. Usually choppers
are made from nodules or pebbles of flint or other
suitable material. Part of the circumference is boldly
flaked into a sharp, if irregular, working edge.

GRAVERS (French=*burins*) (Fig. 4). This tool family, whose members occur chiefly in upper palaeolithic industries, is of very great importance. For a tool to be classed as a graver it is necessary that it should have at least one graver facet. Let us consider what this means. When secondary work is done on a blade or flake as, for example, when an edge is to be trimmed, vertical[1] blows are dealt on the edge, the flake or blade itself being held horizontally. This is invariably the case, as a moment's thought will show. In the case of a graver, however, a vertical blow is dealt at the point of the blade or flake down the length of the implement which is itself held vertically. The resulting flake scar, which truncates the edge of the blade or flake, is known as the graver facet. Before accepting a graver as such, therefore, it is necessary to be sure that there is at least one graver facet present, the existence of which can be demonstrated or not according to the position on the suspected facet of the negative bulb of percussion and the surrounding rings.

The classification of gravers is a matter of some controversy. They can be classified according to type, or they can be classified according to the method of their manufacture. Neither of these systems is perfect, and indeed, the student must always remember that he is not making rules for prehistoric man, but deducing laws from facts. He is in the position of a grammarian, not of the inventor of a language. Though prehistoric man certainly seems from time to time to have desired to make different shaped gravers in different ways, gradations between these so-called types certainly do occur, and hard and fast divisions are all

[1] For convenience it is considered that all blows are dealt from above downwards in a vertical direction.

very well when the selected specimens exhibited in museum series are considered, but in the field intermediate varieties are also found. On the whole, as far as this book is concerned, the older system of classification by types rather than by methods of manufacture will be adopted, as up till now it is the one usually found in the literature of the subject. It depends on whether the working edge of the graver is like a screwdriver (Fig. 4, 6) or like a gouge (Fig. 4, 3). Several subdivisions within each of these classes are distinguished according to the formation of the other side of the working edge, the one side of which is formed by the graver facet. Sometimes this just consists of another graver facet, in which case the working edge is formed by the intersection of two graver facets; at other times it is seen to be a trimmed edge, and so on. At this point it will perhaps be easier to tabulate the different varieties (see p. 65), and briefly to describe them.

Ordinary gravers. When the blade or flake is thin, one burin facet on each side of the working edge is sufficient to make an effective tool (bec-de-flute, Fig. 4, 1), where the blade or flake is thick two or more facets parallel to one another and in the same plane may be necessary either on one side only (single facetted, Fig. 4, 2) or on both sides (double facetted) of the working edge. Naturally this working edge will no longer be as even as when the tool was formed by the intersection of two graver facets only, as it is almost impossible to make the various facets absolutely parallel and in the same plane. But though the working edge may appear slightly irregular when examined, the student should have little difficulty in assigning the graver in question to the screwdriver rather than to the gouge class.

Angle gravers. These have trimming on the other side

of the working edge to the graver facet. When the trimmed edge is at right angles or nearly so to the longer axis of the blade or flake, the term "transverse" is given. Where its direction is inclined at an angle to this longer axis, the term "oblique" is applied. The trimmed edge itself in both cases may be straight

Gravers made on blades or flakes	Screwdriver type	Ordinary	Bec-de-flute Single facetted Double facetted
		Angle — Transverse	straight trimmed concave trimmed
		Angle — Oblique	straight trimmed concave trimmed convex trimmed (parrot beak)
		Single blow	On broken end of a blade On a naturally pointed flake
	Gouge type	Polyhedric	
		Angle — Transverse	straight trimmed concave trimmed
		Angle — Oblique	straight trimmed concave trimmed convex trimmed
		Single blow	On a broken end of a blade On a naturally pointed flake
		Beaked	With stop notch Without stop notch
		Flat	
Gravers made on cores	Screwdriver core graver Gouge core graver (prismatic)		

(Fig. 4, *4*) or concave (Fig. 4, *5* and *7*), and in the oblique variety also convex (Fig. 4, *8*), but not of course in the transverse variety, as no working edge would result. If the student will draw for himself a transverse convex angle burin, he will at once see the truth of this statement.

Single blow gravers. It frequently happens that the broken end of a blade where it has snapped across, or the pointed end of a flake lend themselves admirably to the manufacture of a graver. In each case nothing but the striking of a single blow to make the graver facet is required to complete the tool (Fig. 4, *6*).

Polyhedric gravers. Here a number of graver facets are required, inclined at an angle to one another, in order to produce the convex curve of the gouge. There is generally a hollow on the opposite side formed by a large negative bulb of percussion at the top of a graver facet on the inner side of the working edge (Fig. 4, *3*).

Gouge angle gravers. These are rarely found, but are theoretically subdivisible in the same way as are the screwdriver angle gravers, the difference being that the working edge is here a gouge, and not a screwdriver, and it is therefore necessary that several graver facets inclined at an angle to one another should be struck off in order to produce the curvature of the edge the other side of which is, of course, trimmed (Fig. 4, *9*).

Gouge single blow gravers. These tools are similar to the screwdriver single blow gravers except that, the working edge being curved, several graver facets are again required to form it. The name "single blow" is thus of course a misnomer, but it helps to show the connection between this type of tool and the single blow screwdriver variety.

Beaked gravers. With these tools the "business end" consists rather of a little nose than of a hollow gouge. It is formed by the intersection of a number of little facets with a single large graver facet, from which they curve away to the opposite edge of the blade or flake, thus determining the nose. Fluting technique is the rule for these little facets and the resulting tool is often

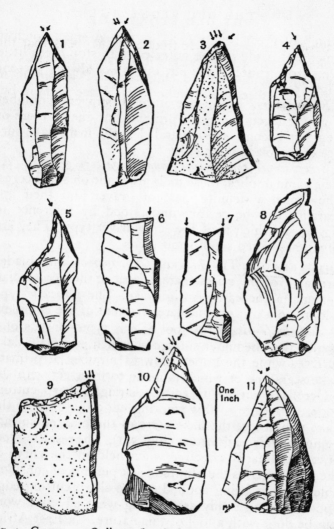

Fig. 4. Gravers. 1, Ordinary (bec-de-flute). 2, Single facetted ordinary. 3, Polyhedric. 4, Oblique straight angle. 5, Oblique concave angle. 6, Single blow. 7, Double transverse concave angle. 8, Parrot-beak (= oblique convex). 9, Gouge angle. 10, Beaked. 11, Core.

a thing of great beauty (Fig. 4, *10*). A small notch is sometimes made on the outer edge to stop these little facets from running too far, but is not always present (Fig. 15, *7*).

Flat gravers. In the case of the flat gravers, a number of graver facets are again present, but one or more of them has become nearly parallel to the main flake surface of the blade itself (Fig. 15, *5*).

Screwdriver core gravers and gouge core gravers. As their name implies, these tools are made on small cores. They form a definite class of graver and their appearance can be readily understood by reference to Fig. 4, *11*, which is of the screwdriver type. They are sometimes called small hand picks.

KNIFE BLADES. The *Audi* and *Châtelperron* knife blades form an evolving series characteristic of the Périgordian element in the early Aurignacian. The *Gravette* type belongs to a distinct and later element of the complex.

Audi knife blades. A tool of this type consists of a small flake, the under surface of which is a plain flake surface, while the upper shows a number of primary flake scars one of which is made to intersect with the under flake surface to form a straight sharp cutting edge. Opposite to this working edge the back of the flake is blunted, the flake scars of the blunted surface being rough and irregular (Fig. 5, *1*). The resulting tool is extraordinarily effective when held in the curve of the first finger as the blunted back permits of considerable pressure being applied on the sharp cutting edge opposite. It is really astonishing what effective work can be done with a tool of this nature. In East Africa experiments have been tried, and with just such a tool made from a natural glass known as obsidian a buck has been skinned in an incredibly short time.

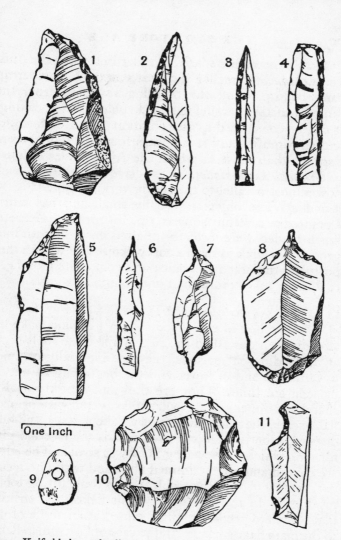

Fig. 5. Knife blades, awls, disc, etc. 1, Audi knife blade. 2, Châtelperron knife blade. 3, Pointed Gravette knife blade. 4, Square-ended Gravette knife blade. 5, Very late Magdalenian variety of Audi knife blade. 6, Awl. 7, Double-ended awl. 8, Awl and end-scraper. 9, Pierced stone ornament. 10, Disc. 11, Notched blade.

Châtelperron knife blades. Similar in form to the Audi knife blade but smaller and neater is the Châtelperron variety (Fig. 5, *2*), the blunting resulting from the removal of tiny parallel flakes. Typologically speaking, it can be considered as an evolution of the Audi knife, and stratigraphically it is always found in more recent deposits than those in which the Audi knives occur.

Gravette knife blades. These have the blunted back now almost parallel to the sharp working edge (Fig. 5, *3* and *4*). The object is usually small and has either a pointed or carefully squared tip. Two or more Gravette knife blades were probably hafted in a longitudinal groove in a stick to form a sort of knife and we can thus postulate the first appearance of a composite tool, i.e. a tool made up of more than one component part.

LEVALLOIS AND CLACTONIAN FLAKES (Fig. 6, *2* and *1*). The method of manufacture of a Levallois flake has already been described (p. 46). While these tools occur at many different periods, they are especially common towards the end of lower and the beginning of middle palaeolithic times. They are thin and roughly oval in shape, the upper surface is flat and covered with primary flake scars, the under surface is a flake surface, the bulb of percussion is often visible and so is the facetted platform on which the severing blow was struck. The edges are curved and often trimmed all round with fine secondary working, with the result that an oval cutting tool is produced. In the case of Levallois flakes, the striking platforms are prepared, and inclined at an angle of 90° to the main flake surface. In the case of Clactonian flakes (p. 117) no Levallois flake and tortoise core technique is involved, the striking platforms are not facetted and are inclined at an angle of 120° or so to the main flake surface, and are made by a swinging-blow technique.

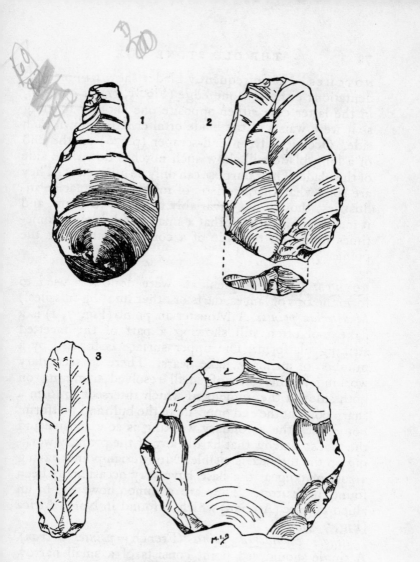

Scale about 2/3

Fig. 6. Flake-tools, etc. 1, Clactonian flake. 2, Levallois flake showing facetted striking platform. 3, A blade. 4, A small tortoise core.

NOTCHES. Not infrequently blades show trimmed indentations either on one edge (Fig. 5, *11*) or on both, in the latter case either opposite one another forming as it were waists in the blade or alternating down each side. Occasionally an end-scraper (p. 76) on the end of a long blade will show such notches down the side of the blade. Their purpose can only be guessed at. They are somewhat characteristic of middle Aurignacian industries, though not invariably confined to them, and it may be remembered that a small notch is even sometimes found on the side of a coup-de-poing near the point.

POINTS. (These implements were doubtless used to form the tips of lances, darts or other hunting missiles.) *Mousterian points.* A Mousterian point (Fig. 7, *1*) is a flake tool often still showing a part of the facetted striking platform. The upper surface is formed by a number of primary flake scars. There is secondary working in the form of small resolved trimming on both sides of the implement which intersect to form a sharp point at the end opposite to the bulb and platform. Sometimes the secondary working is so extensive and the tool so narrow that hardly any of the primary working on the top face is visible. Mousterian points having a sort of tang at the base have very occasionally been found in Europe. They are common, however, in an allied culture (Aterian) which is found in North Africa (Fig. 7, 5).

Single shouldered points (French = *pointes à cran*). A single shouldered point consists of a small narrow pointed blade with secondary trimming at the butt end which carves out a definite half notch and so produces a shoulder. This type appears at the end of Aurignacian

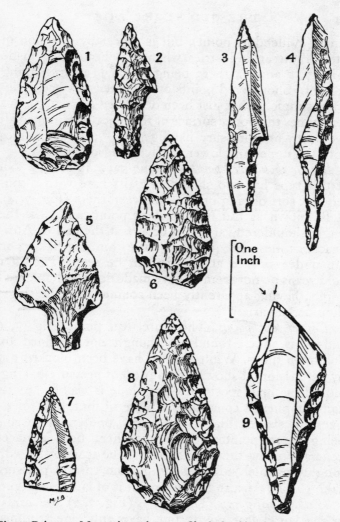

Fig. 7. Points. 1, Mousterian point. 2, 3, Single shouldered Solutrean points. 4, Font Robert point. 5, Aterian point. 6, 8, Solutrean laurel leaves. 7, Portion of Solutrean willow leaf. 9, Late Aurignacian Font Robert point which, having been broken, was reworked into an ordinary graver in Magdalenian times.

times (Willendorf point), but is especially common in later Solutrean industries when it is beautifully made (Fig. 7, *2* and *3*), there being much pressure flaking present. Shouldered points of this later date are sometimes simple, as has just been described (Fig. 7, *3*), but sometimes the upper surface of the object is trimmed all over with fine pressure flaking (Fig. 7, *2*), sometimes both the upper and lower surfaces are so trimmed.

Double shouldered points. As the name implies, a tool of this type has two shoulders at its base with a consequent sort of tang or stalk between them (Fig. 7, *4*). It is known as the Font Robert point, and, like the single shouldered variety, it occurs at the end of Aurignacian times. Frequently a little thinning flaking on the under surface at the tip can be seen. The later Solutreans do not seem to have made double shouldered points, having apparently been content with the single shouldered variety.

Laurel leaf points. The laurel leaf point (Fig. 7, *6* and *8*) is much found in, though not confined to, Solutrean times. While it must have been blocked out by percussion, it shows a great deal of pressure flaking, indeed in small specimens this alone is visible. As its name implies, it consists of a piece of flint, thin for its size and shaped like a laurel leaf, one end as a rule being more pointed than the other. Both surfaces generally show the long narrow flake scars often with roughly parallel sides resulting from careful pressure flaking. The African Stillbay point is of laurel leaf type.

Willow leaf points. These tools (Fig. 7, *7*) are similar to the laurel leaf points but have only one trimmed face—and even here the trimming is sometimes confined to pressure flaking down the sides—the other being a flat flake surface.

ROSTROCARINATES. Tools of this type are found in tertiary deposits, but are also occasionally seen with coups-de-poing of lower palaeolithic date. According to the late R. Moir an evolutionary series from this type to that of the coup-de-poing can be demonstrated, but possibly the latter is rather a development from roughly trimmed and pointed pebbles which often occur with primitive coups-de-poing. For convenience, however, the rostrocarinate is here classed as belonging to a separate family. Essentially it consists of a nodule of flint having an upper and a lower flat surface (the dorsal and the ventral planes respectively) and a pointed or beak-like working end (Fig. 11, *1*). If a Canadian canoe be cut in half amidships and turned upside down one would have something recalling in general shape, though of course on a gigantic scale, the rostrocarinate tool-form.

SCRAPERS. *Side-scrapers.* Side-scrapers are flake-tools especially common in Mousterian times, but occurring also in industries of lower palaeolithic date. Their essential characteristic is the possession of a sharp cutting or scraping edge formed along the side of a suitable flake by the intersection of the main primary flake surface with a number of small flake scars resulting from secondary working (Figs. 8, *1* and 12, 2). This working edge is somewhat convex, except in the case of a very thin variety which is sometimes known as the "cutter". The convexity is clearly an essential feature; anyone trying to scrape a skin with a sharp, straight edge would soon find that the ends of the working edge of the tool would get stuck in the skin and would tear it. In the case of the Mousterian side-scraper the secondary working is of the resolved variety and little characteristic half-moon shaped flake scars can be seen.

End-scrapers. As their name implies, the working edges of these tools occur on the ends of flakes or blades (Fig. 8, *2* and *3*). They are sharply convex and, as before, result from the intersection of the main flake surfaces below with a number of flake scars which, when there is a central keel, frequently rise up fan-wise to meet it (Fig. 1 5, *4*). Sometimes much fluting occurs, especially in middle Aurignacian times. The sides of the flake or blade are themselves often trimmed, but this is possibly to make them less brittle, or perhaps, if the tool were mounted in the end of a hollow bone, to render it less likely to damage the haft. The edges, however, are not as a rule actually blunted. Nevertheless care must be taken by the student to distinguish between such trimming and secondary working definitely intended to produce a sharp cutting edge.

Core scrapers. These tools (Fig. 8, *7*) look like little cores, the working edge being produced by the intersection of somewhat irregular flutings with a flat plane surface below made by the removal of a flake.

Keeled scrapers. In this case the flutings are narrow, flat and regular, and they rise up fan-wise to a point on the keel of the flake or core on which the tool is made and the whole forms an implement of extreme beauty which apparently even flint knappers to-day find a difficulty in imitating (Fig. 8, *6*). Like the beaked graver the keeled scraper is characteristic of the middle Aurignacian period, and a little thought will enable the student to realise that a connection between the two can be shown to exist. Both are made with the same wonderful technique, but in the one case (beaked graver) the business end is made on the thickness of the blade, in the other (keeled scraper) on the breadth of it.

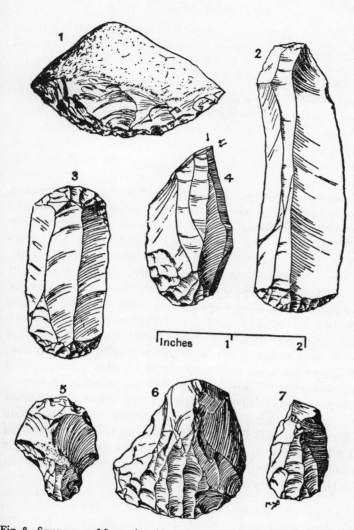

Fig. 8. Scrapers. 1, Mousterian side-scraper. 2, 3, End-scraper and double end-scraper on blades. 4, End-scraper and graver on a flake. 5, Nose scraper. 6, Keeled scraper. 7, Core scraper.

Nose scrapers. The essential feature of these tools is that the scraping edge forms a small nose at the end of a flake, blade or small core defined on each side by a carefully trimmed notch (Fig. 8, *5*).

Round scrapers. Sometimes small, circular or oval flakes are sharpened nearly all round by careful trimming. These are called round or thumb scrapers.

BONE TOOLS

Bone and similar materials such as horn, antler and ivory, were seldom used for tool-making purposes until upper palaeolithic times. We do find, however, in middle palaeolithic industries horse and bison toe bones (Fig. 12, *3*) which show marks of bruising and cutting. They are known as utilised bones, and it is thought that they were employed in much the same way as are anvils. Up to the present it has been assumed that the tool in process of manufacture was held in the one hand while blows were rained on it with a hammer stone held in the other. It is thought possible, however, that Mousterian man when engaged in making such fine secondary working as is found on some of his side-scrapers and points may have rested the flint on something while knapping. If the substance on which the flint rested was not resilient, but hard like a piece of rock, there would be a danger that a shattering of the flint might result; but bone being softer the chances of such a calamity would be lessened.

ARROW STRAIGHTENERS, BROOCHES, SCEPTRES, ETC. (French = *bâtons-de-commandement*). In their simplest form these tools consist of a portion of antler with one or more holes pierced through it, these holes being either circular or oval (Fig. 9, 4). Such tools are first found in middle Aurignacian times, but become common in the Magdalenian period, when they are often beautifully decorated. Various suggestions as to their uses have been put forward. It has been considered that they were arrow straighteners, that they were brooches, that they were sceptres, that they were used for making pliable thongs or reins cut from reindeer hide. In the last case the thong would have been passed

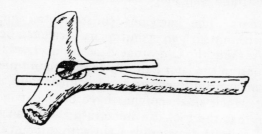

through the hole, held taut at each end, and the tool, slightly rotated, passed up and down it with a stropping motion. It is possible that all these explanations are true. Tools of similar shape are used by modern primitive peoples as arrow straighteners, and the highly decorated examples may conceivably have been used as brooches for holding together heavy skins, or as sceptres, the latter explanation being especially probable in the case of the fine, thin, beautifully decorated specimens which can hardly have been capable of use for any serious work. For the last explanation also modern analogy can be adduced, as similarly shaped tools are used for the purpose in certain parts of Greenland. Further, a moment's thought will show that the wear on the tool in this case would occur on one side of the edge of the hole on the top of the tool, and on the other side of the edge of the hole on the under side of the tool; and in some instances such wear has been noticed.

FISH HOOKS. Little bone fish hooks of various kinds are found in Magdalenian industries. The simplest type consists of a thin needle of bone pointed at both ends with a hole through it, not at the centre. Should a fish swallow it, a stout pull would cause the hook to stick crossways in the gullet of the fish. Other varieties are Λ-shaped; and still more elaborate types occur.

HARPOONS. The harpoons constitute an important family within which an evolutionary series can be recognised. As far as the Old Stone Age is concerned they are only found in the later half of Magdalenian times.

The most primitive type has a pointed stem, up both sides of which small notches have been cut in such a manner that the tool can penetrate a substance easily but can only be drawn out again with difficulty. Later on well made, nicely curved, "detached" barbs are carved on one side of the stem (Fig. 9, *11*), and still later again, these are found on both sides of the central shaft, sometimes opposite one another, sometimes placed alternately (Fig. 9, *9*). At first the barbs remain beautifully curved, but later they become angular (Fig. 9, *2*), and with this development they and their Magdalenian makers disappear. The barbs, especially in the later varieties, frequently have a line engraved upon them. Some people have thought that poison was rubbed on the barbs and that the engraved lines assisted in this matter; others have considered that the engravings were of a purely decorative nature. At the base of the harpoon there is an arrangement for attaching it to a haft. In the Magdalenian industries of France this takes the form of a raised collar round the

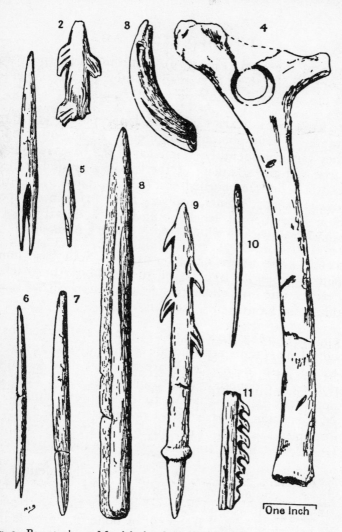

Fig. 9. Bone tools. 1, Magdalenian forked base lance point. 2, Fragment of late Magdalenian (6) harpoon. 3, Pierced horse-tooth ornament. 4, Bâton-de-commandement. 5, Double bevelled butt lance point. 6, Middle Aurignacian split base lance point. 7, Single bevelled butt lance point. 8, Polisher. 9, Magdalenian (6) double barbed harpoon. 10, Needle. 11, Fragment of Magdalenian (5) single barbed harpoon.

base of the stem (Fig. 9, 9), while in northern Spain more usually there is a small protuberance at one side of the stem with a hole pierced through it.

BONE LANCE POINTS. Bone lance points are thin wands of bone pointed at one end. At the other end they vary considerably. Some have their bases rounded, large, flat and spatulate. Others have a single bevelled end or a double bevelled end (Fig. 9, 5 and 7). Little lozenge shaped points, also very finely made, occur too. Some varieties of lance point have a dorsal groove running down the whole length of the specimen.

SPLIT BASE BONE LANCE POINTS. Split base bone lance points are typical of the middle Aurignacian period. The butt ends are split up a short distance, no doubt for hafting purposes (Fig. 9, 6).

FORKED BASE BONE LANCE POINTS. Forked base bone lance points must not be confused with the above. In this case the butt ends are not split, but Λ-shaped notches are definitely carved out (Fig. 9, 1). They do not occur in Aurignacian times and only appear in Magdalenian industries. As a rule in early Magdalenian examples the sides of the notch are almost parallel, in later Magdalenian times they become more divergent.

NEEDLES. Needles only occur in Magdalenian industries. Sometimes they have eyes (Fig. 9, 10), sometimes not. It would seem probable that they were made by grinding a small fragment of bone in a groove in a piece of sandstone or some such hard rough substance. The eyes must have been pierced with fine flint awls. In size needles vary greatly, both small fine and long coarse varieties being known.

POLISHERS. One end of the bone of these tools is rubbed down until it resembles the edge of a spatula. It is impossible to say with certainty for what purpose they could have been used (Fig. 9, 8).

SPEAR THROWERS. Such tools as these are still used by a number of modern primitive peoples. Essentially they consist of a long flat piece of bone with a little projection on the upper side at one end. The other is held in the hand in such a way that it points backwards over the shoulder of the operator and a projectile can be rested upon it with its butt end touching the knob. A sharp turn of the wrist of the operator causes the projectile to be sped on its way, and apparently with some skill a good aim can be made. In Magdalenian times such spear throwers are of no great size, but are often beautifully decorated with figures of animals, etc. (Fig. 19, 1).

WANDS. These are rounded rods of bone pointed at one end and occasionally grooved along their length. They are often decorated. Their exact use is unknown, but for many purposes they must have been convenient.

Chapter V

GEOLOGICAL PROBLEMS

As prehistory, particularly during its early periods, is so intimately connected with geology, it is necessary to say a few words upon this subject where it bears upon our own. Geology, the study of the earth, can be divided into a number of different sections, each having separate names. Thus the study of rocks, though a branch of geology, is called to-day petrology, the study of fossil animals palaeontology, the study of fossil plants palaeobotany, and so on. The history of the earth, the sequence of events that have taken place, is the province of stratigraphical geology, and it is with this branch of the subject that we are more particularly concerned.

The stratigraphical geologist has described the history of the world in five volumes and an introduction. Each of these volumes can be subdivided into chapters, and these again into smaller subdivisions. With the introduction (pre-cambrian times) we, as prehistorians, are not concerned. Apparently life had not yet appeared on this globe, at any rate in the area with which we are dealing. With the first volume (palaeozoic) and its various chapters (cambrian, ordovician, silurian, devonian, carboniferous, permian) we are also not concerned. Although living organisms of many kinds abounded neither man nor indeed even the mammals had yet been evolved. It was during the carboniferous chapter that our coal measures—the source of much of Great Britain's wealth in the past—were laid down, but no man was there to see the process going on.

PLATE III

View of the Pin Hole cave, Creswell Crags.

View up the valley from above the cave of Bouichéta.

Neither does the next volume (mesozoic) comprising several chapters (triassic, jurassic, cretaceous) give any record of humanity. This was the great age of the monstrous reptiles whose remains are so often seen in the galleries of our geological museums. These beasts were in their prime the kings of creation indeed, and the mammals were only just being evolved, slowly perfecting perhaps their superior method of blood supply which, among other things, was destined to help them supplant their scaly predecessors as winners in life's race. It was during the last (cretaceous) chapter of this volume that the chalk cliffs of south-eastern England were deposited below the level of the sea to be raised up later as a result of earth movements.

The third volume (tertiary) contains four chapters, the eocene, oligocene, miocene and pliocene. It is of some importance to us as prehistorians, for it would appear likely that during the period covered by the last chapter man himself actually made his appearance, that at this time, or slightly earlier, the Rubicon was crossed, the purely animal state left behind and a start made on the long road towards our unknown and still unapprehended goal.

It was during the eocene chapter that the London clay, on which the metropolis is built, was deposited in a broad estuary. The climate then seems to have been considerably warmer than it is to-day, and while no traces of man or his handiwork have yet been found, there can be assigned to this period lemur-like animals that lived in trees and have been considered as perhaps remote links in the chain of the human pedigree. The next chapter, the oligocene, tells us little of interest for our particular study. Certain gravels in the east of the Isle of Wight were deposited, but again no remains of man have been found. Strata of miocene date are absent from this country as the area was a land surface and deposition therefore was not taking place. This chapter records, however, much earth movement, and it was now that the Himalayas and the Alps were up-raised. And still nowhere have we yet found any relics left by man. But the last chapter is of very considerable interest to us. Deposits of this age are by no means common, as once again large areas of the earth's surface were land and deposition was not taking place. We are fortunate, therefore, in having a series of important pliocene beds in our own country. The largest area where they occur is in East Anglia, roughly speaking from the valley of the Stour in Suffolk to Weybourn west of Cromer in Norfolk. They consist for the most part of shelly sands and gravels, sometimes rather limey in constitution, known locally as "crags". Frequently fragments of shells make up most of the material. These crags seem to have been laid down in a shallow sea where tides and currents had full play. Pliocene deposits also occur in patches (high level gravels) on the Downs of East Kent. They are found at a considerable height, up to 600 feet above sea level, a fact which suggests that there has been considerable land movement, i.e. changes in the relative level of the land and sea, since their deposition.

The fauna found in the pliocene beds is of consider-able interest. While the greater number of the inverte-brates belong to species still existing, the vertebrate remains are of species now mostly extinct, though many of the genera still survive. The study of the mollusca shows that the climate, at first rather warmer than it is to-day, became successively colder and colder until finally arctic conditions set in. Thus while in the early beds 26 per cent. of the mollusca are warmth-loving, in the later beds none of these persist; and on the contrary, while only 1 per cent. mollusca found in the early beds are northern cold-loving varieties, this percentage increases to 33 per cent. in the latest deposits.

In East Anglia the pliocene and early pleistocene deposits have been classified and the following subdivisions are usually recognised.

	Southern mollusca	Northern mollusca
Weybourn crag ⎱ Chillesford beds ⎰	—	33 %
Norwich crag	7 %	32 %
Upper Red crag (Butley)	13 %	23 %
1 _____		
Red crag	16 %	11 %
Coralline crag	26 %	1 %
Lenham beds		

[1] The horizontal line indicates the start of the pleistocene in E. Anglia. It has now been fixed at the base of the Villafranchian = Calabrian beds in Italy.

With the Lenham beds we are not concerned, but in the Coralline crag, the Norwich crag, and especially the base of the Red crag, in what is called the detritus bed or Suffolk bone bed flints have been found which, it is claimed, have been chipped by man. These are the first human industries known (see next chapter).

With the deposition of the Cromer Forest series we pass on to the period covered by the fourth (quaternary or pleistocene) volume of geological history. This period, most important of all from the prehistorian's point of view, covers and was coterminous with what is known as the Great Ice Age, during and in spite of which palaeolithic man continued to flourish. The climate of western Europe was very different from what it is to-day and more than once actual arctic conditions prevailed. But before going further it will not be out of place to say a word or two about the Great Ice Age and its origin, although, in spite of the immense amount of research which has been devoted to this problem, very little definite information is as yet available.

To begin with, the term "Great Ice Age" is in some ways a misnomer; there was not really one ice age but several, a series of glacial maxima between which warmer periods occurred—warmer, in one case at any rate, than is our own climate to-day. There are two distinct questions which must be considered: the cause of the ice age as a whole and the cause of this periodicity within it. The problems are complicated from many points of view. In the first place it has not yet been shown for certain that an ice age in the northern hemisphere was always contemporary with one occurring in more southern latitudes. Further, actual glaciation is found only in high latitudes or altitudes as the general lowering of the mean annual temperature, even during glacial maxima, was not more than a few degrees, and while, for example, ice sheets covered parts of England and stretched out into the plains bordering the high mountain masses of eastern France, elsewhere and in the south there was little or no actual glacial activity. It is thus important to keep in mind the latitude under discussion when considering phenomena due to a glacial maximum. Ice phenomena, such as occur throughout the year around the North Pole to-day, obtained much further south it is true, but there was no ice near the equator, except on the tops of high mountains.

Various explanations, geographical and astronomical, have been put forward to account for the facts. It has been claimed that drastic alteration in the levels of land and sea, the elevation of high mountain masses in Scandinavia and elsewhere, coupled with slight earth movement in Florida of such a nature as to cause a diversion of the Gulf Stream from the shores of western

Europe, would be sufficient to produce the necessary fall in temperature. England lies on the same latitude as Labrador, yet the climate of the two regions is vastly different: a diversion of the warmth-giving Gulf Stream, coupled with ice sheets that would have formed in the hypotheticated high land regions, would undoubtedly have considerably altered our climate. Yet this explanation seems to be quite inadequate; for one thing it only applies to western Europe, and similar glacial phenomena occur in America and in many other parts of the world. Again, there is no particular reason to believe that any of these geographical changes that are thus postulated ever did take place, and they hardly could have occurred without leaving tell-tale evidence behind them. Finally, these geographical changes fail completely to explain the periodicity within the Great Ice Age, i.e. the succession of glacial maxima with warmer inter-glacial periods between them.

The astronomical explanations are two-fold. The first, Croll's hypothesis, depends upon the precession of the equinoxes and the fact, demonstrated by astronomers, that in past ages the earth's orbit round the sun, which is now nearly circular, was formerly very elongated, this change in the orbit from an elongated ellipse to a nearly circular one being periodic. A possible combination of these two phenomena would undoubtedly result in a situation when, owing to the precession of the equinoxes, the northern hemisphere would be turning away from the sun—in other words the sun would appear to be low in the heavens as it is with us in winter—at the same time as the earth was at a vast distance away from the sun at the farthest end of its elongated elliptical orbit. In such a case the very great distance of the earth from the sun, coupled with the fact that its rays would strike the northern hemisphere obliquely, would undoubtedly have given rise to extremely cold winters, little compensated for by the corresponding short, though very hot, summers. A change round due to the precession of the equinoxes, even when little alteration had taken place in the eccentricity of the earth's orbit, would mean that the northern hemisphere, although in winter still far from the sun, would face it —the sun would now be high in the heavens—and this would compensate to some extent for the loss of heat due to the great distance from its source. At the same time the short summer, although hot, would be cooler than in the first instance, because now, although close to the sun, the latter would be low in the heavens and many of its rays would be reflected off and not absorbed and changed into heat.

That these phenomena did indeed sensibly affect the climate of quaternary times is almost certain, but the whole problem cannot be explained on Croll's hypothesis alone. For one thing the effect would never be seen at the same time in both hemispheres, and if ice ages occurred in both they would not be contemporary but complementary to one another. While, as has been said, it is extremely difficult to prove anything in this matter, evidence resulting from work in South and East Africa and elsewhere tends to show that the climatic changes which took place there in the form of alternating pluvial and dry periods corresponded to and were contemporary with glacial and inter-glacial alternations in the north.[1] This evidence is

[1] It must be remembered that during an ice age for glacial phenomena to have occurred there must have been considerable precipitation to allow of the formation of the glaciers and ice sheets. While a dry glacial maximum, i.e. one in which there are no ice sheets or glaciers and therefore

of an archaeological nature and depends on the discovery of industries apparently belonging to the same cultures in the two areas; for example, if comparable datable industries are found in connection with a pluvial deposit in one area and with a glacial deposit in the other, it becomes very difficult not to equate the pluvial period and the glaciation. While it is true that cultural and time sequences are not necessarily contemporary, such a lag in time between the two cultures, as it would be necessary to postulate should the pluvial not be more or less contemporary with the glaciation, would be well nigh unthinkable. Croll's hypothesis is to-day somewhat under a cloud, but it must not be forgotten, even if it does not explain everything. It is quite likely that the Great Ice Age of quaternary times was not the result of any one cause but was due to the concatenation of a variety of circumstances which chanced to be cumulative in their effect.

As mentioned above, a second astronomical explanation has been suggested, and this did indeed receive considerable support.[1] It is considered that the positions of the poles themselves have varied; and that the sun is a variable star, the amount of heat which it gives off not being always constant and that during quaternary

no ice phenomena, is possible, glaciation did occur at certain times in northern Europe in pleistocene times. In southern latitudes precipitation, which in cold climates would swell the ice sheets and the glaciers, would simply fall as rain, the temperature never falling to freezing point owing to the latitude. It follows, then, that pluvial periods in the south must be the equivalent of glaciations in the north. But, of course, apart from other evidence a pluvial period in the south need not be contemporary with a glaciation in the north unless precipitation was contemporary in the two areas.

[1] See an interesting publication of Dr G. C. Simpson, C.B., F.R.S. "The Climate during the Pleistocene Period", vol. L, *Proc. Roy. Soc.* Part III (No. 21), Session 1929–30.

times it went through two complete cycles. A combination of these facts, it is suggested, is sufficient to explain most of the phenomena which we have observed. Taking as an example a locality near Frankfurt it is argued that the shifting of the poles would lower the mean annual temperature by some 5° and that this would be enough to produce an ice age. The other phenomenon postulated is used to explain the periodicity of glacial and inter-glacial stages. Implicated in Dr Simpson's theory, would be the occurrence of a dry glacial stage, i.e. a glacial maximum without sufficient moisture to admit of glaciers being formed, between two warm inter-glacials which themselves are flanked by normal glacial maxima. Whether such a dry glacial stage can be shown to have existed seems as yet uncertain, the onus is now on the glacial geologists to re-examine the phenomena in the field in the light of Dr Simpson's suggestions. But there is very little doubt that the shifting of the poles which seems within certain limits to have taken place, must have played a very important rôle in the formation of our Great Ice Age.

The number of glacial maxima which actually have occurred remains a matter of dispute. Dr Albrecht Penck, who investigated the glaciations of the Alps and whose colleague, Dr Obermaier, continued the work in the Pyrenees, claim that there have been four which were named Gunz, Mindel, Riss and Würm (Fig. 10), after four little rivers flowing down the northern side of the Alps into the basin of the Danube. The intervening inter-glacial stages were named Gunz-Mindel, Mindel-Riss, and Riss-Würm respectively. They further suggest that after a slight amelioration of climate (Achen stage) following on the Würm

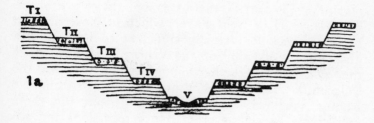

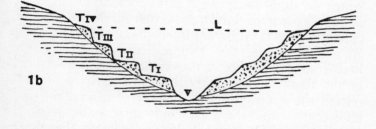

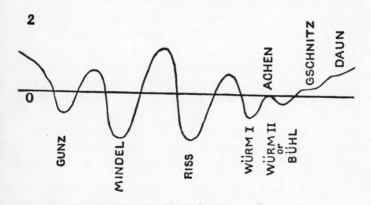

Fig. 10. Geological diagrams. 1*a*, Normal river terrace system showing step formation of the under topography. 1*b*, River terrace system due to incomplete erosion of a valley previously filled with morainic material (p. 96). 2, Penckian scheme of glaciations.

maximum (Würm I), there was a slight return of the ice (Würm II or Bühl stage[1]) which in those regions, however, was not actually sufficient to form a fifth glaciation. Following on the Würm II or Bühl stage they also note two further minor oscillations (called the "Gschnitz" and "Daun"), due to the retreating ice having remained stationary for a period; but these oscillations as well as other minor recessions and advances of the ice do not concern us here, having been either too slight to be of any but very local importance, or having occurred during post-palaeolithic times. They recognise that the different inter-glacial stages were not all equally warm, the Mindel-Riss having probably been considerably hotter than either the Gunz-Mindel or the Riss-Würm. Other investigators have not admitted the validity of this scheme of glaciations and have claimed that there were only three arctic maxima, while the late Dr Bayer of Vienna asserted that there had only been two.

Clearly the geography and latitude of the area in which the investigator works will influence his conclusions: the further north he goes the less evidence for an inter-glacial period will he obtain, for a rise of temperature which may have just been enough to produce an inter-glacial stage in more southern latitudes may have been insufficient to make any apparent difference in the north. Thus, in East Anglia—the area being fairly northerly to begin with, and under the influence of great ice sheets from the Scandinavian

---

[1] The term "Würm II" (generally used in this country rather than Bühl) should not be confused with the same expression which Penck has used to represent what he considers to be a return of the ice after a slight recession (Laufen) in the middle of Würm I times, a phenomenon, however, which seems to be of little but local importance.

mountains in addition—the evidence for the various inter-glacial periods is far less marked than in the Pyrenees district, and in view of the fact that the various inter-glacial stages were by no means all equally warm, it is not at all impossible that when the evidence in such localities is examined one or more of them may be found to be almost non-existent. However, at the moment Penck's scheme holds the field as a sort of framework into which information on glacial matters has to be placed; but it is quite possible, nay probable, that modifications will have to be made in the future.

During quaternary times there were considerable local earth movements, and these have been especially examined in the eastern and southern parts of England, where raised beaches of pleistocene date are found— sometimes far inland, as at Chichester. About the middle of the period there appears to have been here-abouts a sinkage of the land relative to the sea averaging nearly 100 ft.; subsequent elevation of the land brought back the relative levels almost to their original positions, but the physical effects of these movements have to be taken into account and have complicated matters con-siderably for the prehistorian when he attempts to cor-relate the archaeological and geological records. Raised beaches around a country are not necessarily all of one age, even when they are at about the same height above sea level. There may have been differential earth move-ments. Thus our southern English raised beaches are pleistocene in date, and very much older than apparently similar ones which can be seen in Scotland.

Before passing on to the last and most recent volume of geological history, it might be well to describe briefly some of the effects of glacial activity which the prehistorian encounters in the field, especially in this country.

BOULDER CLAYS. Perhaps the most typical glacial deposits that are met with are the so-called boulder clays or drifts. Several different boulder clays have been recognised. They are by no means all alike in appearance or constitution. For the most part, however, they consist of tough unstratified clays containing angular lumps of chalk, flint and various other fragments of rocks that have been torn off and carried over the country by moving ice sheets. This material was left at the bottom of the ice sheet when it could carry it no further, and actually formed a *moraine profonde*. A study of the nature of these fragments of rocks is of extreme importance, as the petrologist is often able to say whence they were torn off by the ice; and thus can be determined the direction from which came the glacier or ice sheet responsible for the drift.[1] Naturally, if the ice happened to pass over a deserted human settlement site, some of the tools that had been dropped by man would also be caught up in the drift, and such "erratics" have been discovered. Incidentally the student will at once recognise, now that the nature of a drift is understood, that any artifacts found in a drift must necessarily be older than the age of the drift containing them.

Moving glaciers and ice sheets tend to scratch and groove the rocks over which they pass, and as the direction of the flow of the ice is constant these scratches and grooves are necessarily more or less parallel. Equally rocks in the drift which have escaped being ground up to powder are frequently themselves ice-scratched, but as their position in the drift may have varied from time to time, the ice scratches in this case are not by any means necessarily parallel. In the same way flint implements when they become incorporated as "erratics" in a drift are often covered with such scratchings.

[1] Analysis of the contained minerals also helps in this respect.

LOESS. Normal glacial maxima necessarily coincide with periods of considerable precipitation and each maximum is flanked, as it were, by periods of cold, dry steppe conditions. At these times there was deposited on hill and dale a sand-like wind-borne material known as loess. Two such loesses are clearly distinguished in north-eastern France, flanking the chief maximum of the Würm glaciation (Würm I). They are known respectively as the older and the younger loesses.

RIVER TERRACES (Fig. 10). When walking along a river valley one sometimes notices terraces which run at various heights along the side of the valley and usually "grade" more or less with the valley bottom, that is to say the terraces rise slowly with the valley bottom as one travels inland from the sea. In this connection it should be noted that old beach lines which once formed the verge of some ancient lake now disappeared, as well as beaches at the margin of what was once an estuary of the sea, but is now, owing to earth movement, raised above sea level, do not so grade but are strictly horizontal. Again, lateral moraines, the result of glacial erosion and subsequent deposition along the sides of the valleys, also occasionally have the appearance of terraces and these do, of course, grade to some extent with the valley bottoms. But even a superficial excavation will at once reveal their morainic origin and it is thus easy to distinguish them from true river terraces.

On examination river terraces are found to be composed of gravels, and as these frequently contain industries the history of their formation and their date are of considerable importance to the prehistorian. A river flowing down from highland country to the sea exerts a certain amount of energy and is able to do a certain amount of work. This work will consist in carving out its bed both vertically and laterally, in other words in deepening its channel and cutting away its banks, subsequently removing the material, which it carries down to the sea there to be re-deposited. The amount of energy that a river can display, the amount of work it can do, depends upon two factors: (i) its velocity, and (ii) its volume. The velocity of a river depends on the slope of the valley, the steeper the slope the greater the velocity. Suppose a river capable of denuding its bed and transporting materials down to the sea has its velocity checked by earth movement, i.e. by a sinking of the land relative to the sea, instead of being able to carry the materials out to sea it will now deposit them further inland; instead of denudation aggradation will set in and spreads of gravel will be deposited. Suppose, however, that fresh earth movement again takes place in the opposite direction and the land rises relative to the sea. The velocity of the river will increase again, denudation will set in afresh, and most of the gravel spreads will be removed and carried out to sea. But as a rule traces of gravel will remain along the sides of the valley and thus river terraces are formed. It can readily be imagined, therefore, that several such terrace systems could result from a series of slight alterations in the levels of land and sea.

The same phenomena can result from alterations in the volume of the river without there having been any change in its velocity. During a glacial maximum in a given region most of the available moisture was solidified, and as it were locked up in the form of glaciers and ice sheets, and this would mean a diminution in the volume of water in the local rivers. Consequently a deposition of gravels would result. On the other hand, with the coming of inter-glacial times and the rapid melting of the ice, the volume of the rivers must have been vastly increased, and much of the deposited gravel would be denuded away. Thus, as before, a series of river terraces might easily be formed.[1] As far as eastern and southern England are concerned it would seem likely that both these causes operated, and it is not always easy in any given instance to differentiate between them.

An important fact should not be missed by the student when considering river terraces. A single terrace is composed of gravels, etc., that have been laid down by river action and it follows therefore that the geological law of superposition holds good, i.e. that the top layers of any terrace are newer in date than those at the bottom. But taking the terrace system as a whole each step results not from aggradation, i.e. building up, but from denudation, viz. cutting down by the river, and it follows, then, that the law of superposition, which only applies in the case of aggradation, must be reversed; that the top terrace must be the oldest and the bottom terrace the youngest (Fig. 10, *1a*). This fact should be carefully noted as it is of great importance when correlating the archaeological and geological records.

Again, when studying river terraces it is important to take into account the under topography of the valley, that is the shape of the ground below the surface deposits. Should this show a step formation, then the

[1] In mountainous districts it frequently happens that towards the heads of the valleys moraines occur, and lower down, beyond the limits reached by the glaciers, normal river terraces. A definite transition between a moraine and a river terrace can often be observed and thus a particular river terrace system can sometimes be correlated with the local scheme of glaciations.

gravel terraces on these steps were no doubt formed in one of the foregoing orthodox ways. On the other hand, if it is found that the under topography of the valley is U-shaped (Fig. 10, *1 b*) and shows no step formation, then it may have happened that, on the retreat of a glacier or from some other cause, the valley had become completely · filled with débris, and that this later has been mostly removed by successive deepenings of the river bed, leaving a series of terraces at various points along the valley side. In this case it will not be true to say that the top terrace is the oldest and the bottom the newest since all the terraces are merely the relics of a single infilling of the valley. Actually the bottom terrace, being composed of the first fillings of the valley, will be the oldest, and the top terrace, being composed of the last, will be the newest. Once again the geological law of superposition holds because we are dealing with a case of aggradation that has merely been exposed for us by the denuding action of the river. At first sight these matters seem very complicated and difficult to grasp, but the moment the student understands the simple principles on which they are based he will have no difficulty in visualising and comprehending the whole matter.

We now come to the last volume of the geologist's history of the earth. This (the recent) has not yet been closed; our history to-day is being written therein. With the end of quaternary times western Europe underwent rapid changes of temperature with the result that the fauna and flora were also considerably modified. Changes took place, too, in human cultures and palaeolithic times came to an end. With the story outlined in this volume, therefore, we are not here concerned. During the time covered by the earlier portions of it most of our peats and river alluviums were deposited, and a study of these has been of inestimable importance to the prehistorian interested in the later branches of his subject, helping him to determine the relative dates of the different cultures and their correlations with datable geological deposits.

Finally, the reader may well ask whether or no any information as to the actual age in time of the various glaciations can be hazarded. Since, as will be shown later on, correlations between datable industries and the glacial deposits can be made, it would follow that if the glacial deposits themselves could be in any way dated in terms of years some idea as to the antiquity of the various cultures would be attained. A number of attempts have been made to arrive at some conclusion in this respect; to find, for example, the actual date of the last glaciation. A. Heim, basing his estimate on the present rate of growth of the delta deposited by the Muotta in the Lake of Lucerne, concluded that the ice had vanished completely some 16,000 years ago. A more exact method has been devised and carried out by Baron de Geer of Upsala who has actually counted the number of layers of sediment which the ice of the last glaciation deposited during its retreat. These sediments were deposited during the summer thaws, and they cover Scandinavia from south to north like tiles on a roof, each of them corresponding to one year. They are by no means of the same thickness and some of them have special peculiarities by which means the individual layers can be recognised at various sites. Thus from a number of observations the whole sequence of them in Scandinavia from south to north can be determined. The total number should give in years the time taken by the ice in its retreat from south Scandi-

navia to the north; and this number is about 5000.
In the north itself the ice continued to deposit layers
in Lake Ragunda from the moment the lake was un-
covered by the retreating ice. About the middle of the
last century this lake was drained and the number of
layers that have been counted in it amounts to 7000.
It would follow then that the number of years from our
own day to the time when the ice was in south Scandinavia would be 7000+5000= 12,000 years. It would
seem, then, that the ice barrier (? Würm II)[1], which has
left its moraine along the south coast of Norway and,
continuing through Sweden, along the south coast of
Finland, must have existed about 12,000 years ago.
Moraines laid down by the ice in Würm I times occur
considerably further south, and the ice must have taken
some time in retreating thence to south Scandinavia,
probably another 5000 years at least. Thus if we could
go back 17,000 to 20,000 years we should find ourselves in Würm I times, that is in the maximum of the
last great glaciation.

SOLIFLUXION OR SOIL-CREEP. Should the upper
layers of an area which is frozen to a considerable depth
thaw rapidly the resulting water will be unable to soak
away and the upper beds will become sludgy. In the
case of deposits lying on a slope some downward
slipping often results. This phenomenon is known as
solifluxion. The deposits, for example gravels, instead
of being evenly bedded, will show, in section, a festoon-
like structure and many of the pebbles, instead of lying
horizontally, are frequently found tipped up at any
angle.

[1] This cold oscillation became in northern latitudes a veritable
glacial maximum. In certain caves in north Wales, for example, beds
containing upper palaeolithic industries are overlaid by a drift of
Würm II age.

Chapter VI

EOLITHS: THE DAWN OF THE STONE AGE

THE problem of the origin of man has long fascinated inquirers, and, as has already been said, it is rather one for the biologist than the prehistorian. It seems probable, however, that the Rubicon between the animal and the human state was crossed at some moment far back in the third volume of geological history. But stone industries in which specimens occur showing the necessary criteria of human workmanship (p. 49) have not been unearthed from deposits of an earlier date than those of the late tertiary (pliocene) period. Even so, it is clear that an enormous time has elapsed since mankind first appeared on this globe, and many of our former ideas, theological and otherwise, have to be rudely modified when we consider this immense antiquity of our kind. As we have no relics except chipped flints, it might be argued that we have only found evidence for the existence of a tool-making animal in those remote times, yet it is difficult to believe that some unknown animal manufactured often well-made flint tools, in late tertiary times, and yet that this being was not human.

The problem of the existence of tertiary man was first brought forward by the Abbé Bourgeois at a congress at Paris as long ago as 1867. The Abbé had found chipped flints in beds of upper oligocene age near the village of Thenay, south of Orleans. An examination of the specimens had convinced him that the chipping was the result of human handiwork, but most prehistorians were unable to accept his conclusions; and, indeed, they were probably right, as increased knowledge of the ways in which nature fractures flint has demonstrated that the Thenay specimens are probably purely natural. A few years later somewhat similar objects, this time of miocene date, were discovered near Madrid, and 1877 saw the discovery by M. Rames of still further examples, again of miocene age, in the department of Cantal, at Puy-Courny and Puy-Boudiou. From 1899 onwards specimens of like nature were unearthed from plateau gravels of tertiary age near Igtham in Kent by Benjamin Harrison. While none of the former finds are now accepted as artifacts by the majority of prehistorians, a number of serious students believe that the Kent specimens are really the result of human workmanship.

Nothing further happened until 1905 when M. Boule published a long article in *L'Anthropologie* in which he attempted to demonstrate that all the so-called eoliths had been chipped solely by natural forces. His arguments were based on observations made on large mortar-making machines at Mantes, near Paris. He argued that the stones which issued from the machines often showed chipping not unlike that seen on some of the hitherto published eoliths, and that as a mortar-making machine was purely mechanical in its action, it could quite well be paralleled in nature, and that the action of torrents or the sea in chipping flints was analogous to that of the machines at Mantes. It is certainly true that specimens showing a remarkable series of chippings are produced by such machines, but no mechanical machine or natural force can chip a flint, dealing the blows from only two or three directions more or less at right angles to one another. This criterion for apprising human workmanship was not appreciated in 1905, and as a matter of fact no tertiary finds known at that date exhibited it.

M. Boule's attack on the existence of tertiary man was followed up by the Abbé Breuil who showed what wonderful results were produced when pressure of a great weight of super-incumbent "overload" caused differential movements in gravels containing flints. He based his arguments on certain eocene finds near Clare-mont-sur-Oise, and exactly similar specimens have been collected by Mr Hazzledine Warren from the so-called "Bull Head" beds not far from London. Some of these pseudo-implements which Mr Warren has found are really amazing, there being beautiful sharp working edges closely approximating to those found on Mousterian scrapers. But on the other hand once again the specimens will not stand the application of the criterion which has been so often adumbrated. Two years later further finds of flints, apparently chipped by man, were made at Boncelles in Belgium by MM. Münck and Rutot, the gravel beds in which they oc-curred being of oligocene age. Once again, however, there was no absolute proof of their human workman-ship.

In 1910 a fresh investigator, Mr Reid Moir of Ipswich, entered the field with a number of eoliths which he had collected locally at the base of the Red crag. These included objects useful as awls or scrapers, together with a new type of tool which was named the "rostro-carinate" (Fig. 11, 1) and a few core-tools. Essentially, however, the industries are of the flake variety. Several well-known scientists were converted by Mr Moir's discoveries to a belief in the existence of tertiary man, the most prominent among them being the late Sir Ray

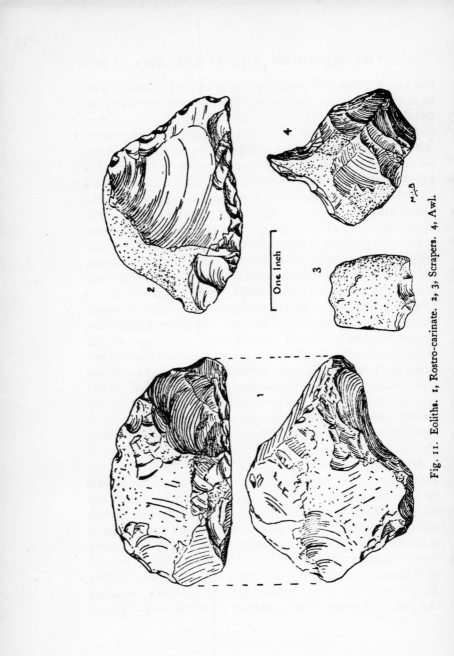

Fig. 11. Eoliths. 1, Rostro-carinate. 2, 3, Scrapers. 4, Awl.

One Inch

Lankester. But Messrs Breuil and Boule, who came over to see the finds, still maintained their sceptical attitude. Mr Moir, however, was undaunted and continued his researches at new sites until finally at Foxhall, a few miles from Ipswich, he collected a series of specimens of such a nature that an examination of them by M. Breuil caused him to change his ideas completely and to join the ever-growing company of those pre-historians who believed in the existence of man as early as late tertiary times. Even now, however, there are still some prehistorians of note who believe that the East Anglian finds are solely the result of natural causes. Yet biologists, on totally different grounds, have long claimed that tertiary man must have existed.

One result of these diametrically opposed opinions has been the twofold use of the word eolith which has grown up. Originally coined from eos = dawn and lithos = stone, as a name for the earliest of human in-dustries, it had a respectable connotation. Later it was used, and still is by those who do not believe in the tertiary finds, as a term of contempt to denote purely natural specimens bearing a certain resemblance to humanly worked tools. Thus a piece of rock, even of palaeozoic age, happening to possess a naturally chipped cutting edge would be classed as an eolith. I would emphasise that the original use of the term should be retained and that the word eolith should only be used for specimens which are considered to be artifacts. At the present time, however, it is necessary to be sure which meaning of the word an author intends to convey to his readers when he uses the term.

As has been said, the most important finds of eoliths in Europe have been made in the "crags" in East Anglia. Of course this is not to be taken as an indication that East Anglia can be considered in any way as the site of the Garden of Eden! But the number of sites in western Europe, where suitable tertiary deposits occur in which the investigator might expect to find the work of man, is not large. Most of the area at the time was land and suitable deposits which, in process of formation, might contain and preserve artifacts were very rare. The importance of this part of England is therefore obvious and a more detailed, though brief account, of the East Anglian finds in tabular form, showing the position of the various beds, will not now be out of place.

At Thorington Hall bivalve shells with the hinges still intact have been collected from just above the artifacts. This is very important evidence for the prehistorian, as no subsequent differential movement of the gravel, such as might have caused fracturing of the contained flints, can have taken place, since it would certainly have led to the smashing of the delicate hinges of these shells. Incidentally, too, at this site, as well as at Foxhall, the deposit in which the specimens occur is of a sandy nature and not packed with pebbles. So even if differential movement had occurred no fracturing due to the pressure of one stone against another could have resulted. Of course this argument does not apply to earth movements that have elevated or lowered large tracts or regions without there having been any differential movements of the deposits at any given site. The whole country might have risen or fallen without the hinges of the shells getting smashed, but any differential movement in the gravels would have destroyed them.

At Foxhall the chipped flints were found at two different levels only, and this can be best explained if

Sequence of the later pliocene and first pleistocene deposits in East Anglia

First pleistocene
{
Cromer Forest series
Weybourn crag
Chillesford beds
Norwich crag
Upper red crag (Butley)
}
} Arctic climate

} Cold climate

Late pliocene
{
Red crag with the detritus or
Suffolk bone bed at its base [1]
Coralline crag
}
} Cool climate

Warm climate

Sections (not to scale) of three important sites near Ipswich.

Bramford Pit, 2½ miles N.W. of Ipswich	Foxhall, 3½ miles east of Ipswich	Thorington Hall, Wherstead, 2 miles south of Ipswich
Glacial deposits. 6 ft.	Middle glacial gravel. 12 ft.	Traces of glacial gravel and boulder clay
Middle glacial gravel. 4 ft.	Iron stone. 6–9 ins.	
		Shelly Red crag. 18 ft.
Crag sands (marine) 10 ft.	Red crag sands. 3 ft.	
Detritus bed = level of ancient land surface. 1 ft. (implementiferous)	Implementiferous floor at 16 ft. below surface	Bone bed = implementiferous layer
	Nodule bed. 3 ft.	London clay
Early tertiary deposits containing no traces left by man. 15 ft.	Implementiferous floor	
	Red crag sands	
	Nodule bed	
	Sands	
Chalk	London clay.	

Red Crag

[1] The detritus bed is composed largely of the sweepings of an old land surface which for a time formed the beaches and hinterland of a pliocene sea. Most of the eoliths come from this layer.

we consider that these levels were actually old land surfaces on which man lived, in other words that we are dealing with "floors" or actual occupation sites.

The argument that the flints were chipped elsewhere by natural forces and later incorporated in these late pliocene gravels cannot always be maintained. Small flakes, as well as large specimens, occur together and this would not happen under such circumstances, as the selective action of flowing water would cause the smaller and lighter specimens to be collected together at one site and the larger and heavier objects at another. At the same time it does seem probable that some of the chipped flints are considerably older than the deposits in which they are found, as they show scratchings, possibly the result of ice action, which not only occur on natural faces of the flint but are also sometimes found on flake scars which are considered to be the result of human chipping. Indeed, it may prove in the long run that humanity is still older than late pliocene times and that some of the tools had been manufactured before the formation of the "crags". At what period the scratchings took place, and whether indeed they are due to ice action, is still a matter of controversy. At the end of pliocene times there is a noticeable change in the Molluscan fauna, and the succeeding earliest pleistocene beds show a steady fall in the general temperature in East Anglia until, at the close in Weybourn crag–Chillesford beds times, veritable arctic conditions prevailed. This very cold period has been correlated with the Gunz or first glacial maximum of Penck mentioned on page 88.

It will be seen, then, that while the existence of tertiary man seems incontestable many problems still remain to be elucidated. So far the evidence rests solely on the occurrence of chipped flints which in some cases satisfy the criteria for human workmanship. Certain highly mineralised fragments of bone found in the tertiary deposits have been considered by some investigators to have been pointed by man for use as awls. While this was, of course, quite probably the case, the state of preservation of the bones is such as to have destroyed all absolute evidence that they are really artifacts.

So far no human remains have been discovered associated with the chipped flints in the East Anglian beds. Comparisons with the early human remains so far found in Java or China would anyway be out of place as these distant regions will probably be found to be distinct provinces not racially connected with our Western European folk, even should they be more or less contemporary with them which, indeed, is not quite certain.

Chapter VII

EARLY PLEISTOCENE TIMES AND CULTURES

THE eoliths which were discussed in the last chapter come from deposits of late tertiary age.[1] We pass on now to quaternary or pleistocene times throughout which, in suitable localities, our early forerunners contrived to flourish, leaving behind them their implements of stone which we shall now proceed to study. Nor did these by any means all belong to one culture, even before the latter part of the period when Aurignacian man entered our area and introduced the so-called upper palaeolithic cultures. These, however, will be considered in a separate chapter; our concern now is to give an account of the different cultures which occurred and of the conditions under which they flourished before the Aurignacians arrived on the scene.

Before going further, then, it will be well to describe the industries belonging to the various cultures which can be distinguished. Later we shall discuss their distributions, relationships and origins.

CROMERIAN INDUSTRIES. No one walking along the foreshore at Cromer in Norfolk can fail to notice at low tide immense spreads of large flints. This material has mainly been derived from a stone bed which lies just below the Weybourn crag in the cliffs behind. To-day both the crag and the stone bed at Cromer are completely buried beneath an accumulation of beach talus, but the former is visible low down in the cliff at Weybourn itself, a few miles along the coast. Hunting about among the flint of these "spreads" a searcher can not infrequently find artifacts. For the most part these consist of large flakes carefully struck off from

---

[1] As already noted the eoliths themselves are mostly much older than the late pliocene deposits in which they were found. Some of them might actually date back to pre-pliocene times.

a core, the striking platform being unfacetted and frequently inclined at a high angle to the main flake surface. Although there is not always any further trimming a sharp cutting edge has often been obtained. In colour the specimens are generally bright orange. Occasionally more finished tools are found and rarely specimens of a core-tool type such as choppers, etc. have been collected. Essentially, however, it is a flake industry with which we are dealing. It has been suggested that these Cromer sites were workshops and that therefore finished tools are not present. But there seems no particular reason to consider that this mass of flakes was purely débris, many of them may well have been implements and the larger ones could certainly have been very effectively used as chopping tools.

It would appear that these chipped specimens were made by men who lived at a time when the earlier beds of the Cromer Forest series were being laid down, for a few undoubted artifacts have been discovered in them, and the horizon at which they occur probably represents the ancient land surface on which these makers of the Cromerian industries wandered, collecting the raw material for their tools from exposures of the stone bed below. Actually most of the Cromer Forest Bed is now also masked by talus.

CHELLEO-ACHEULEAN INDUSTRIES. The following subdivisions of the Chelleo-Acheulean culture have been made, determined partly on stratigraphical, partly on typological grounds.

Chelleo-Acheulean	Acheulean	Micoquian[1]
		Upper Acheulean
		Middle Acheulean
		Lower Acheulean
	Chellean or Abbevillian	Upper Chellean
		Lower Chellean
		Pre-Chellean

[1] Named after the little rock shelter of La Micoque near Les Eyzies where the industry was first recognised.

In the gravel terraces of the Somme valley, where a large number of sites have been carefully studied, many further subdivisions have been demonstrated— no less than seven for the Acheulean—but it is doubtful whether such a classification will be found applicable in other regions.

Although some rough side-scrapers, awls, etc., do occur, these industries are almost entirely made up of coups-de-poing which are of course core-tools. A core-tool, it will be remembered, is one which is made by taking a nodule of flint and knocking flakes off it until it becomes the requisite shape, in contradistinction to a flake-tool which, as its name implies, is fashioned from a flake struck off the original nodule. We are thus essentially dealing with core-tool industries, for even when in a later stage of their evolution coups-de-poing were sometimes made from large flakes, they were treated like nuclei and trimmed all over both surfaces so that the implement has the appearance of a core-tool.

The basal type of coup-de-poing was roughly pear-shaped (Fig. 3, *1*), one end being somewhat pointed and the other rounded. The sides of the tool were sharp, though to begin with at any rate the edges were irregular. As a rule one side was sharper than the other. The butt end was sometimes sharp, but sometimes quite blunt. In fact not infrequently it was hardly trimmed at all, the natural cortex of the flint being left untouched—a feature common in lower Chellean times. To begin with, free-flaking was mostly employed in its manufacture, both surfaces of the flint being covered with large irregular flake scars. At a later stage in the evolution of the tool (to some extent in upper Chellean, but predominantly in Acheulean times) the edges become more regular, trimming becomes neater and a considerable amount of secondary, resolved, flaking can be seen. Later again the tool becomes flatter and more tongue-like at the pointed end. Not only is one side blunter than the other, but frequently on the blunt side a small platform is left about a third of the way up from the butt, or a blunted area is made by a sort of battering of the side. At this time (Acheulean), too, the primary free flaking gives place largely to controlled flaking (Fig. 2), and the edges are very neatly and skilfully made. Still later on (upper Acheulean and Micoquian times) the implements become small and dainty and are sometimes made on flakes, the main flake surface either partially or wholly remaining (Fig. 3, 2).

Another rather different evolution from the basal type can also be recognised, leading to the development of oval coups-de-poing, generally known as ovates (Fig. 3, 3). These are essentially Acheulean implements. As their name implies, they are not pear-shaped but oval. Trimmed all over, as before, they undergo an analogous evolution to that already outlined for the pear-shaped variety. Once again we can observe the introduction of controlled flaking and finally the appearance of small neatly made varieties of the tool (upper Acheulean).

It may be noted that while a section through the middle, both of the pear-shaped and the oval types, is generally oval, it is occasionally plano-convex. In other words one face is trimmed flat, the other being very convex. This variation is common in upper Chellean and lower Acheulean times. Again, when the edges of either the pear-shaped or oval coups-de-poing are looked at head on, they are sometimes seen to be twisted like an elongated S or Z, a phenomenon known as the S or Z twist (Fig. 3, 3). It is as if somebody had held the bottom half of the tool firmly in one hand and then the other had slightly rotated the top half either to the right or left. The S or Z twisted coup-de-poing does not appear till Acheulean times.

Throughout much of Chellean times, as also during the early and late Acheulean, warm conditions obtained and we find the remains of great herds of the warmth-loving, straight-tusked elephant (*Elephas antiquus*), as well as of the soft-nosed warmth-loving rhinoceros (*Rhinoceros Merckii*). In the rivers lived hippopotami, and there was also the great sabre-toothed tiger (*Machairodus neogæus*), as well as many other warmth-loving beasts. One of the most typical mollusca of this period was a minute shell-fish called *Corbicula fluminalis* which itself can stand but little in the way of cold. Before Chellean times the fauna was somewhat different and many species survived from the pliocene period. The middle Acheulean was mainly a cold time and, as might be expected, a mixed fauna flourished. Many of the older warmth-loving species survived, but new and cold-loving types such as the mammoth appear as well. After Acheulean times came tundra conditions and the Mousterian culture, with reindeer abounding in western Europe.

Throughout much of the pleistocene period considerable local earth movements took place and if we could go back to Chellean times we should find that not a little of our geography would have to be re-learned. The Irish Channel and the English Channel were non-existent and land stretched westwards from Ireland for a long distance. No North Sea acted as a barrier to the spread of cultures, and it has been claimed that the Mediterranean consisted of two small lakes, the Adriatic being non-existent. On the other hand a broad gulf stretched up northwards from the Caspian Sea. How

PLATE IV

Venus of Lespugue, Venus of Willendorf and Venus of Unter Wisternitz.

ever, by the end of Mousterian times we should find
that conditions had become more normal.

CLACTONIAN INDUSTRIES. Clactonian industries are
often found in the same gravel beds as coups-de-poing.
Roughly speaking they are contemporary with the various
phases of the Acheulean culture. They consist, however,
for the most part of flake-tools (Fig. 6, 1). Almost invariably the flakes have been struck off from an unfacetted
striking platform which is found to be inclined at an angle
of about 120° to the main flake surface. Small chopping
tools, rough scrapers and discs are found as well as worked
nodules of flint, etc. Although in some ways different a
certain affinity with the earlier Cromerian industry can
be perhaps detected. In Belgium a similar industry is
generally called Mesvinian. The well-known industry
which was found in a red loam at High Lodge near
Mildenhall, Suffolk, and which was formerly classed as
Mousterian, is really a late and highly evolved Clactonian.
Finely trimmed side-scrapers and pointed tools occurred.

TAYACIAN INDUSTRIES. Coarse industries of small
flake tools roughly contemporary with the late Acheulean and first recognised at Tayac near Les Eyzies
should here be mentioned.

LEVALLOISIAN INDUSTRIES. Here again we have to
deal with flake industries. Found in western Europe
associated with coups-de-poing of lower, middle and
upper Acheulean date, and with the Mousterian, they
consist of side-scrapers, points and of course of Levallois
flakes (p. 70, and Fig. 6, 2) and these vary considerably
in size. In the Somme valley a large number of subdivisions of the Levalloisian (no less than seven) have
been determined, mainly on stratigraphical grounds;
though how far this detailed zoning will be found
applicable in other regions remains yet to be seen. The

early tools are considerably more roughly made than those of later date. Among the true Levalloisian tools there also occur in the later subdivisions, possibly as a result of contact with Acheulean tool-makers, cordiform coups-de-poing (Fig. 12, 1).[1] A sort of Mousterian point and discs are frequently found, and throughout we naturally get tortoise cores (Fig. 6, 4) in abundance.

The earlier Levalloisian industries are found with the remains of a non-arctic fauna such as is typical of Acheulean times, and they have sometimes been described as the "Warm Mousterian".

MOUSTERIAN INDUSTRIES. (Fig. 12). The implements of pure Mousterian industries are mostly flake-tools. Typical among them are side-scrapers, points, Levallois flakes, discs, etc. Utilised bones, too, are frequently found. The industries, when both their typology and the methods used in their manufacture are taken into account, are very characteristic. Facetted striking platforms are common and the secondary working, made by step chipping and leaving quantities of small, squat flake scars, is very typical. Actual bone tools of Mousterian date are almost non-existent, but Professor Breuil has described a bone spear-head of Mousterian date from Castillo, and two other bone tools have been cited by Dr Henri Martin from La Quina, Charente.[2]

True Mousterian industries occur but rarely in open stations. The climate was becoming very cold, indeed arctic, and reindeer abounded, so the Mousterian tool-makers naturally preferred to live in rock-shelters. In the Dordogne district of France no hard and fast line can be drawn between the end of Acheulean and the beginning of Mousterian times, for layers containing Mousterian tools together with the remains of a rein-

[1] Cordiform coups-de-poing with S or Z twists do not seem to occur.
[2] A few Mousterian bone tools have also come from Creswell Crags.

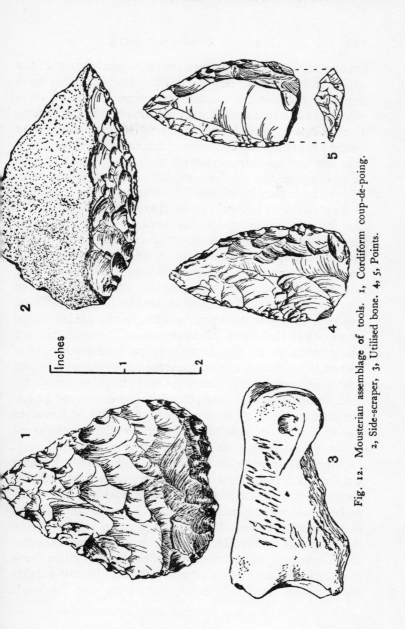

Fig. 12. Mousterian assemblage of tools. 1, Cordiform coup-de-poing. 2, Side-scraper. 3, Utilised bone. 4, 5, Points.

deer-including fauna occur immediately above those
which have yielded late Acheulean implements. To a
large extent the Micoquian industries may be considered as the result of contact between the two cultures,
as thus transitional between them, though in no sense
do they represent an evolution from the one to the other.
It is not improbable, however, that the Micoque coup-
de-poing was the product of Acheulean workmanship
under the influence of the Mousterian new-comers.

The Mousterian culture in these districts is usually
divided into three stages—the upper, middle and lower.
Early Mousterian tools show a distinct Levalloisian
influence and the cordiform type of coup-de-poing
abounds. Very early Mousterian layers, however, have
been discovered at Combe Capelle where this type of
tool is absent, but occurs in immediately overlying
deposits of lower Mousterian date. It is perhaps true
to say that the early Mousterians of France did not
bring with them the cordiform coup-de-poing; it is
more likely that on arrival they copied those which they
found in use in the districts they had invaded. By
middle Mousterian times, however, these more Leval-
loisian-like types of tool, including the large Levallois
flakes and so on, had disappeared from the industries,
and we find only side-scrapers, points and discs, etc.
In upper Mousterian times the implements became
smaller and somewhat monotonous, consisting almost
entirely of little side-scrapers and points. A characteristic site where such an upper Mousterian industry
occurs is the rock-shelter of La Quina in the Charente.
Throughout Mousterian industries there are also occasionally found balls of flint which some authorities think
may have been used as bolas stones. Many further
subdivisions of Mousterian industries can be made

locally, but such local classifications are seldom of wide significance.

The Mousterian culture is usually classed as middle palaeolithic. As will already have been perceived and as we shall see more clearly in a moment, however, it would seem an error so definitely to separate it from the cultures responsible for the other flake industries already described. The word "Mousterian" has been used very loosely to describe any early flake industry, and the result has been confusion. Properly speaking, Mousterian industries are those which it is considered were probably the handiwork of members of the Neanderthal race (p. 131). Though in various parts of the world somewhat similar flake industries occur, it is by no means correct to class them all as Mousterian. They may all belong to the same flake-tool civilisation, but they are not necessarily all the product of the same culture.

DISTRIBUTION, RELATIONSHIPS AND ORIGINS OF THE FOREGOING CULTURES (Figs. 13 and 14). Having briefly mentioned the various industries of pleistocene date prior to the arrival of the Aurignacians, a word must now be said as to their distribution. The Cromerian industry need not long delay us. So far it has not been found much beyond the limits of the locality where it was originally recognised. This does not necessarily imply that the culture was of East Anglian origin. This flake industry is of a simple kind, and it is perhaps the rather peculiar orange-coloured appearance of the flakes themselves and their great size (only possible in an area where large nodules of flint occur naturally) which makes this industry so characteristic.

The coup-de-poing industries on the other hand are

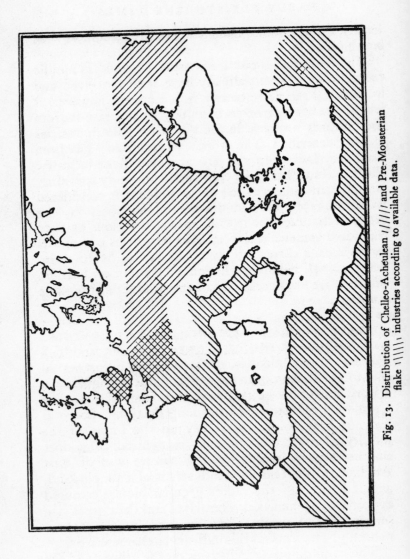

Fig. 13. Distribution of Chelleo-Acheulean ////// and Pre-Mousterian flake \\\\\\ industries according to available data.

very widely spread. They are found all over Africa, being abundant in South Africa, where the name "Stellenbosch" is given to them. Beautifully made examples sometimes made of obsidian (a difficult material to work) have been unearthed in Kenya, and they are found throughout North Africa. Examples, too, have been collected in the modern tin mine workings at Jos in Northern Nigeria. They have been found in Palestine and Transjordania and again in large numbers in the Madras Presidency of South-east India. Recently, too, some specimens have been collected from near Bombay. In Europe, however, they are limited almost entirely to the extreme west of the continent. Hardly any have been discovered much to the east of the Rhine. A few examples, it is true, belonging to the heyday of their development, have been found in Poland, and at one or two other isolated sites; but practically speaking they are absent from northern, central and eastern Europe, as also from Asia, north of the Eur-Asiatic backbone of mountain masses.[1] In Spain and central Italy coups-de-poing occur, and it should be observed that those regions, as also Palestine, are close to Africa. But elsewhere in western Europe coup-de-poing industries abound, being especially common in north-east France, southern Belgium and south-east England.[2]

[1] In spite of the extremely refractory materials from which the tools are made, the industries associated with *sinanthropus* and the other early pleistocene skeletons found in northern China are essentially of the flake, not core, variety.

[2] In this country coups-de-poing have been cited from East Devon, Somerset, Dorset, Wiltshire, Hampshire, Isle of Wight, Sussex, Kent, Surrey, Middlesex, Berkshire, Gloucestershire, Worcestershire, Oxford-shire, Buckinghamshire, Hertfordshire, Essex, Suffolk, Norfolk, Cambridgeshire, Huntingdonshire, Bedfordshire, Northamptonshire, Warwickshire and Nottinghamshire. Certain finds from Yorkshire have also been claimed as of this date, but the matter is still uncertain. The main concentration of finds, however, is in the south-eastern counties.

East of the Rhine where industries occur, which from
a comparison of the associated fauna can be dated as
contemporary with the coups-de-poing industries further
west, the tools are found to be of the flake variety. As
a typical site Taubach in Thuringia may be mentioned,
but much further work on these flake industries, which
have sometimes been classed as pre- or proto-Mous-
terian,[1] in these areas, and indeed in others further east
—in Russia and northern Asia—is still required.

It is thus probable that as early as lower palaeolithic
times prehistorians will have to distinguish in Europe
at least two distinct civilisations: the one, characterised
by the wonderful coup-de-poing industries being of
African origin, at any rate so far as migration into
Europe is concerned, the other, essentially Asian. In
other words, culturally speaking, the continent of Asia
at that time extended as far west as the Rhine. Cultures
of the second civilisation have given us the various flake
industries, though these are not necessarily in every case
closely interconnected. The flake-tool civilisation seems
to have been much less stable than its core-tool contemporary. Whereas amazingly similar coup-de-poing
industries are found all the way from South Africa to
England, and not only does the same type of tool occur
but its evolution is everywhere similar, a number of
cultures of the flake-tool civilisation seem to have been
readily evolved at different places and at different times.
While in some cases these are doubtless interrelated we
have no choice, until the possible connecting links are
more fully understood, but to consider them as to some
extent independent. Perhaps the Clactonian culture[2] is
in part the result of contact of the two civilisations,

[1] The Tayacian occurs in Palestine immediately below the late
Acheulean and in Turkey a flake industry occurs in gravels near Ankara.
[2] If, indeed, it is a true culture and not merely a technique.

...tfication in the Cromer District.	Stratification of the upper Thames Terraces, Oxford Dist. (simplified)	Stratification at the Traveller's Rest Pit, Cambridge
..ND SUBSOIL BROWN BOULDER CLAY GRAVELS Caught up in the Brown Boulder Clay are a number of upper palaeolithic implements presumably of the same age as this gravel.	ALLUVIUM 'REINDEER' LEVELS OF THE SUNK CHANNEL = Würm II EVENLY BEDDED GRAVELS partly capping the Summertown—Radley Terrace (a)	SOIL AND SUB-SOIL BROWN LOAM In this layer a few flakes have been found. EVENLY BEDDED GRAVELS No fauna or industries known.
..ARTH AND PART OF ..MER-HOLT RIDGE = ..R CHALKY BOULDER ..Y ..rickearth occurs in a ¼ mile from West ..ton to the left of the ..mer road. Bunter ..les occur. Some ..eul tools occur as ..tics in the Ridge, ..ch was formed during ..Riss glaciation. ..NDS AT WEST RUNTON ..Acheul coup-de-poing ..rred here.	SOLIFLUCTION LEVEL below (a) and capping the Wolvercote Terrace. = Würm I	TWISTED GRAVELS AND LOAMS AND OCCASIONAL THIN BAND OF LOAM This deposit is clearly disturbed by ice action. A few very late Acheulean, blue-patinated implements have been found.
	WARM OCHREOUS GRAVELS OF THE SUMMERTOWN-RADLEY TERRACE AND THE WOLVERCOTE CHANNEL, middle and late Acheulean coups-de-poing occur. = Riss-Würm	EVENLY BEDDED SANDS AND GRAVELS This deposit has yielded a 'warm' fauna. A number of weathered Chellean and lower Acheulean, brown patinated implements have been found. At the base occur a number of sandstone boulders showing ice scratchings due doubtless to some glaciation earlier than the evenly bedded sands and gravels.
..ROMER-HOLT RIDGE, ..A BOULDER CLAY = ..ASTERN BOULDER CLAY ..ulder clay is to be seen ..pit behind West ..ton.	ARCTIC BED AT BASE OF THE WOLVERCOTE AND SUMMERTOWN-RADLEY TERRACES. Riss	
..GRAVELS ..t top of the Cromer ..Some early Leval-..ools are claimed from ..e gravels.	WARM GRAVELS OF THE HANBOROUGH TERRACE (90 ft.). Mindel Riss.	
..TED DRIFT AND TILL ..NG DOWN INTO THE ..IC UPPER CROMER ..ST BED ..late Chellean tools ..as erratics at the ..of the Till.	BOULDER CLAY OF THE COTSWOLD PLATEAU (up to 600 ft.). Mindel age.	
..CROMER FOREST BED ..n climate prevailed: ..Chellean tools occur. ..RN CRAG = Very ..climate.		

GEOLOGICAL PERIOD	SOMME VALLEY (MUCH SIMPLIFIED)	LOWER THAMES (MUCH SIMPLIFIED)	CLIMATE	CROMER AND DISTRICT	PREHISTORIC CULTURES	HOXNE	TRAVELLER'S REST PIT NEAR CAMBRIDGE
WÜRM II = BÜHL	Top Brickearths of St Acheul = Weathered Younger Loess	Slades Green 'Trail'	VERY COLD	Hunstanton brown boulder-clay	Upper palaeolithic tools as erratics		Brown stiff loam
	Younger Loess Solifluxion	Gravels and Halling (Medway) Deposits	COLD	Gravels immediately below brown boulder-clay	Upper palaeolithic		Top evenly bedded gravels
WÜRM I		Sunk Channel	ARCTIC	Brickearth with bunter pebbles and perhaps a part of the Cromer-Holt Ridge	Mousterian	Upper glacial beds	Twisted gravels and loams
		Coombe Rock at Baker's Hole			Levallois V		
			COOL		Early Mousterian	[Late and middle Acheulean coups-de-poing.] Warm lacustrine gravels	(Unconformity)
	Red clay	Taplow terrace					
	Older Loess	100 ft. terrace gravels at Swanscombe	WARM	Top sands at West Runton	Late Acheulean		Evenly-bedded sands and gravels
RISS	Solifluxion 'Infra' sands Solifluxion	Chalky-Jurassic boulder-clay of Essex	VERY COLD	Boulder-clay and major part of the Cromer-Holt Ridge	Middle Acheulean	Basal boulder-clay	Ice-scratched boulders in base of deposit immediately above the gault
	Gravels	Dartford Heath gravels	WARM	Coarse gravels at top of cliffs	Early Acheulean and Early Levalloisian		
MINDEL	Torrent gravels passing down occasionally into a true Coombe Rock	Plateau Drift (in part)	ARCTIC	Contorted drift passing down to the Till and then to Upper Part of the Cromer Forest Bed			
	Gravels		WARM	Lower Cromer Forest Bed	Chellean		
	Solifluxion (? Günz, seen in 45 m. terrace)		ARCTIC	Weybourn Crag			

Chapter IX

LATE PLEISTOCENE TIMES AND CULTURES

THE upper palaeolithic cultures are, as we shall see, quite different from any that have occurred before, and there is no question of any evolution from the Mousterian to the Aurignacian industries in our area. Something quite fresh arrived in western Europe and not only are the industries totally different, but the men who made them in no way resemble their Neanderthal forerunners. For the first time in Europe we find the remains of *Homo sapiens*: our own ancestors now hold sway. Not only do the industries differ completely in detail from those of earlier date, but their general appearance too is quite dissimilar. Upper palaeolithic tools are essentially made on blades and in this they differ from earlier industries where the tools are fashioned from flakes or cores. The difference would appear at first to be but slight, and of course many artifacts of upper palaeolithic date are flake or core-tools and not made on blades. Taken as a whole, however, when an upper palaeolithic industry is studied even cursorily, its obvious dissimilarity from the flake industries that preceded it and the continual presence of blade tools mark it off completely from anything with which we have hitherto had to deal . Furthermore, for the first time, so far as western Europe is concerned, we find a large number of gravers or burins in the industries, and while, in Palestine outside our area, this type of tool has been found as far back as Acheulean times, and while even in our own area it persists well on into the Mesolithic period, it is essentially characteristic of upper palaeolithic cultures, and it is only in industries belonging to them that it occurs in large numbers. It is therefore not inappropriate to describe the industries belonging to the upper palaeolithic cultures as "blade and burin" industries in contradistinction to the "flake-tool" industries of Mousterian and earlier date, and the essentially "core-tool" industries of the coups-de-poing makers. Moreover, now for the first time bone and antler were extensively used for making tools, and altogether there is a much greater variety in the tool types than heretofore. Now, too, for the first time art makes a dramatic appearance among man's activities. In western Europe there are three successive upper palaeolithic cultures (Aurignacian, Solutrean, Magdalenian), the first itself a complex made up of at least three distinct elements.

THE AURIGNACIAN CULTURE. In the Dordogne, on layers containing late Mousterian industries, there rest beds which yield artifacts of quite a different character. A classic site is the rock-shelter of Audi not far from the ruin of the mediaeval castle at Les Eyzies. At first sight the new industry appears to show a very considerable falling off from the beautifully made though somewhat monotonous late Mousterian implements. The tools are, for the most part, rough and poorly made. Many Mousterian types persist. We find a few small coups-de-poing, discs, side-scrapers, Mousterian points and so on, but among these there occur end-scrapers, gravers and above all Audi knife blades (Fig. 5, _1_). In no sense of the word does the new industry represent an evolution from an earlier Mousterian one, but it would seem that the Mousterian culture was weakening rapidly and that new-comers were appearing on the scene. It is to these new-comers apparently that the introduction of the Audi knife blades and gravers was due. Whether at any given locality the industry of these times was made by degenerate Mousterians influenced by the new-comers, or by some of the new-comers moving in and influenced by the Mousterians around them it is difficult to say. The climatic conditions remained very cold and, taken as a whole, the faunal remains are fairly similar to those found in Mousterian times except that now a good many red deer bones occur, which suggest that the surroundings were somewhat less tundra-like. The Audi stage marks but a short transition when the older Mousterians and the new folk co-existed; soon the former disappeared altogether, and the higher culture held sway.

Within the Aurignacian culture five subdivisions have been recognised. These are best given in tabular form, viz.:

Subdivisions	Typical tools
Font Robert stage	Font Robert point (Fig. 7, 4)
Upper Aurignacian	Gravette knife blade (Fig. 5, 3)
Middle „	Beaked graver (Figs. 4, 10 and 15, 7)
	Keeled scraper (Figs. 8, 6 and 15, 4)
	Split-base bone lance point (Fig. 9, 6)
Lower „	Châtelperron knife blade (Fig. 5, 2)
Audi stage	Audi knife blade (Fig. 5, 1)

The lower two subdivisions are nowadays often grouped together as the so-called Périgordian stage, the middle Aurignacian being called the true Aurignacian and the upper two subdivisions the Gravettian. The evidences of stratigraphy and typology confirm this succession. In the industries of the middle (true) Aurignacian new types of tool appear, as shown in the table, but also the fluting technique reaches a standard never before and seldom afterwards attained. This matter will be further considered when we come to deal with the question of the origin of the culture. Throughout Aurignacian times we find, together with the tools typical of the various subdivisions, gravers of all kinds, end-scrapers, awls and so on (Fig. 15). Taken as a whole the blade character of the industry is very marked, except perhaps in the Audi stage, where still the influence of the earlier flake industries predominates. Occasionally when excavating Aurignacian sites, decorated objects have been found and these will be considered more particularly in the chapter devoted to the Home Art: but special mention must be made here of the occurrence of small statuettes made from mammoth ivory or fine-grained rock, which have been found in western Europe, central Europe, Russia and as far east as central Siberia (Plate IV and Figs. 18 and 19), as well, of course, as of the amazing cave art which now appears for the first time and will also be considered in subsequent chapters.

Not infrequently the remains of man himself are unearthed. While these consist sometimes of mere fragments of bone found in the homes, careful or ceremonial burial, sometimes with red ochre, can be recognised in several cases. Thus at Cro-Magnon—a rock-shelter site near the railway station of Les Eyzies —burials of a number of individuals were discovered, some of the skeletons being carefully decorated with necklaces made of sea-shells, though the sea is many miles distant from Les Eyzies. It must surely follow, then, that some interest had been taken in these interments as otherwise it would seem unlikely that the necklaces, which must have been of some value to their owners in those days, would have been buried away with the skeletons.

Two distinct types of human being can be recognised among the skeletal remains found associated with

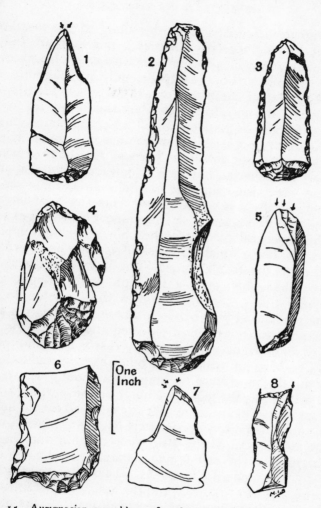

Fig. 15. Aurignacian assemblage of tools. 1, Graver and end-scraper. 2, End-scraper on long blade. 3, End-scraper with trimmed sides. 4, Keeled scraper. 5, Flat graver. 6, End-scraper with side awl. 7, Beaked graver with notch. 8, Upper Aurignacian "Noailles" graver with two notches = small double transverse straight angle graver on blade.

Aurignacian industries. Both belong to the so-called Neanthropic race (*Homo sapiens*), but they are quite different in detail. As representative examples we can cite the finds at Combe Capelle, and Cro-Magnon.

The first of these was excavated by Dr Hauser as long ago as 1909, in a small rock-shelter not far from Montferrand in the Dordogne. An entire male human skeleton of very striking appearance was found lying in an excavation made on purpose for the interment. Early Aurignacian implements occurred around it and there were also a number of shells around the scalp. Anatomically it is very different from any Neanderthal skeleton. There are far less prominent brow-ridges and a high vertical forehead; the chin is well-developed, the jaw being small. The skull is long and narrow, although the face is broad. The individual seems to have been only 5 ft. 3 in. high, with straight and slender limbs. Schliz considers this skeleton to be intermediate in type between that of Cro-Magnon and certain human remains discovered at Brno in Moravia with an Aurignacian industry of east European type.

Cro-Magnon man on the other hand seems to have been tall, his stature ranging from about 5 ft. 10 in. to 6 ft. 4 in.; the legs were longer in proportion to the arms than they are in present day men and the leg below the knee was disproportionately long as compared with the thigh; the hands also were big but the fingers shorter and the palms longer than is usually the case with most modern Europeans. The cranial capacity was large, 1590 to 1750 c.c., and the head dolichocephalic;[1] the glabella brow-ridges were well marked, the orbits

---

[1] All upper palaeolithic skulls are long headed, with the exception of a few Aurignacian examples found in the great rock shelter near Solutré which appear to be on the borderline between dolichocephaly and brachycephaly.

PLATE V

Clay bisons at the Tuc d'Audoubert.

Solutrean relief at Le Roc.

rectangular and low in height, the nose long and narrow, the jaw strong and powerful. If one met a Cro-Magnon man to-day in the street he would appear tall and well-grown, strong and vigorous, but not otherwise very extraordinary. At the well-known cave of Paviland in the Gower Peninsula, South Wales, excavated by Buckland as long ago as 1823, there were unearthed the skeletal remains of a man of the Cro-Magnon type—usually wrongly described as the "red lady of Paviland".

At the Grotte des Enfants, Mentone, two other skeletons of a very different type have been excavated; one, that of an old woman, the other that of a young man. According to Dr Verneau, and other anatomists, these show distinct negroid features. No other examples of this type have been discovered elsewhere in Europe and there seems no reason to consider that they had any hand in the introduction of the Aurignacian culture into this continent. Were they chance emigrants?

The distribution of the Aurignacian industries is very wide (Fig. 16). As far as western Europe is concerned, they are concentrated in the south of France and northern Spain, but are also found in caves in England as far north as Derbyshire, as well as in open stations in the south-east of the country. They have been found in Italy and again in central and eastern Europe where, however, they differ slightly in character from those found further west. Rich deposits containing Aurignacian industries have been unearthed in Palestine, and in East Africa innumerable finds have been made. In North Africa, too, where they are called Capsian, they commonly occur,[1] but in South Africa, although an

[1] In Egypt certain somewhat special upper palaeolithic industries are named Sébilian.

Aurignacian influence is undoubted, industries of this culture have not yet been isolated. In Asia a somewhat peculiar Aurignacian has been cited in Siberia, and even as far east as northern China. In India little pre-historic investigation has as yet been undertaken, except in Bombay and Madras, but a few examples of what in Europe would be classed as Aurignacian tools have been discovered. It would appear, then, from this all too brief survey that at this date the distribution of *Homo sapiens* was very widespread.

This brings us to a consideration of the origin of the Aurignacian culture. Three distinct elements making up the western European complex can be noted. The origin of the earlier (Périgordian) is uncertain. It was perhaps in part influenced by the previous Levalloisian culture, though some prehistorians have postulated a North African cradle. The other two elements seem to have arrived from eastwards. The distinctive middle Aurignacian industries yield tools often made by a fluting technique. Objects of art appear, such as the sculptured Venuses, etc. Neither a fluting technique nor statuettes nor bone tools are found in Africa, but they can be matched from as far away as east central Siberia. It would seem, however, that in western Europe this middle Aurignacian either died out or was submerged by fresh immigration from the east, and we next find the Gravettian[1] dominating the scene. To the east these two components of the Aurignacian are found as distinct cultures, the former being the more northerly in its distribution. The corresponding cultures of this date in northwest and north Africa (early Capsian), in Egypt (Sebilian), in Somaliland and in Kenya are by no means identical with the west European Aurignacian. Though often rich and beautifully made they have

[1] Absent from Palestine, present in Kurdistan.

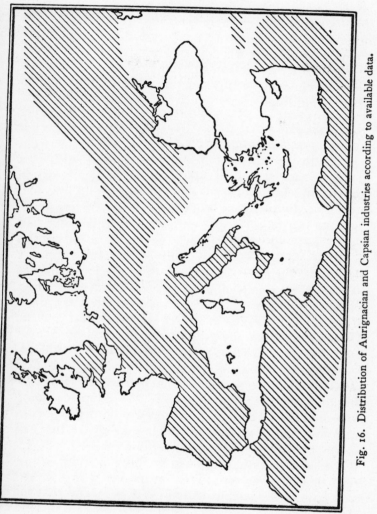

Fig. 16. Distribution of Aurignacian and Capsian industries according to available data.

about them a certain monotony; some pigmy tools occur and, as has been said, there is no sign of any art. On the other hand the fusion with the Périgordian of the culture streams coming successively from Asia to western Europe gave birth to some of the most splendid art and industries known—really amazing when account is taken of the conditions under which the people had to live.

Exactly where to place upon the map the cradles where these three culture-streams originated is not definitely known, but if one did indeed come from Africa perhaps we should look to the Central Sahara, an area now completely desert but then probably much more fertile. Maybe the Asian streams similarly issued from somewhere east of the Caspian Sea or from somewhere in the Gobi Desert? It is more than possible that areas now desert, but formerly fertile, were the cradles of all our bigger cultures. Nor can we say definitely from what earlier culture-stock Aurignacian man was evolved. The occurrences of gravers in an Acheulean milieu near Nazareth in Palestine and the detailed investigations of Leakey in Kenya might suggest that the African element at any rate developed from the Acheulean culture; perhaps as a result of contact with a flake-tool culture penetrating southward from the north? It must always be remembered that Africa seems especially to have been the home of the coups-de-poing makers. This derivation, however, can hardly be postulated for the Asian stream and it may prove that the origin in this case was quite different.

Evidence has been adduced to show that the Mousterian culture was roughly coterminous with the first maximum of the last glaciation (Würm I), and that the Magdalenian culture was coterminous with the second maximum (Würm II). It would seem, then, that the Aurignacian must be assigned to the intervening period (Achen stage) lying between Würm I and Würm II.

But the climate towards the end of Aurignacian times was becoming very cold and dry, as is indicated by the presence of such animals as the saïga antelope, and the Achen stage, especially towards its end, must in no sense be considered by the student as in the least resembling an inter-glacial period.

THE SOLUTREAN CULTURE. The Solutreans broke into western Europe as a horde of invaders. Armed with the laurel and willow leaf lance (Fig. 7, 6, 7 and 8) points, manufactured as a result of their new discovery of pressure flaking, they seem for a time to have completely dominated the scene and yet to have been always aliens. Perhaps one might give as an analogy the invasions of the Philistines into the Semitic world. They seem to have been few in number and while here and there the old Aurignacians must have been driven out or exterminated, elsewhere they probably managed to survive. Solutrean man kept to the plains and seldom penetrated far even into the foothills. He has left us but few traces of his artistic ability if any, but these will be discussed in the chapter on the home art. In some ways, indeed, the Solutrean episode must be considered rather as that of the domination of the older peoples by a powerful caste than as an actual replacing of one people by another.

— The burial places of this date yield skeletons seemingly of the Cro-Magnon type, but further eastwards, whence the invaders came and flooded the west, different types of skeletons of this date have been unearthed.[1] This, of course, is just what one would expect. If several millennia hence excavation was undertaken by future

[1] Perhaps the best of these, not yet properly described, is that found at Klause in Bavaria, where a burial in red ochre has been excavated.

historians in India, the chances of unearthing the skeleton of a European rather than that of an Indian would be remote.

The Solutrean people have left us in caves in the Dordogne and the Pyrenees a plentiful stock of their typical implements constantly to be found in beds resting on those containing industries of the Font Robert stage. The student should not forget, however, that Solutrean industries do not consist solely of tools peculiar to the culture; there are also numerous end-scrapers, gravers and bone tools similar to those found in other upper palaeolithic industries.

A threefold subdivision of the Solutrean culture has been suggested: upper Solutrean, typical Solutrean and proto-Solutrean. The earliest of these only rarely appears in western France but is more common as one goes east-wards, rich deposits having been found in northern Hungary. The proto-Solutrean laurel leaf in Hungary is a much coarser tool than the true laurel leaf of typical Solutrean times in France. It shows much more percussion flaking. It appears in the lowest Solutrean levels in the west of the continent. Typical Solutrean industries are characterised *par excellence* by the presence of finely made laurel leaves, mostly showing pressure flaking throughout. These vary considerably in size from an inch or two in length to as much as a foot. Of course specimens of this size are rarely found, but a cache of immense finely made ones was discovered at Volgu, Saône-et-Loire. A variety of laurel leaf, with the sides constricted towards the base to form a sort of tang is known, and sometimes examples of considerable size have been found. The single-shouldered point (Fig. 7, *2* and *3*) does not occur outside south-west France and northern Spain and even in these parts is only found in, and is the typical tool of, late Solutrean industries. It has been suggested that its presence indicates a weakening of the Solutrean influence and a resurrection of the earlier late Aurignacian culture. It must be remembered that the shouldered point had long previously been developed and it is possible that the Solutrean invaders took over the making of this kind of tool, applying to its manufacture their own special technique of pressure flaking. At one or two places, too, in late Solutrean industries, bone needles have been found, a type of tool which develops especially in Magdalenian times. This, again, may be an indication of the weakening of the Solutrean influence and a sign that it was slowly giving way in southern France before the advance of the Magdalenian culture which seems, in part at any rate, to have been an evolution from the late Aurignacian, in areas where the Solutreans never seriously penetrated.

The distribution of the Solutrean industries (Fig. 17) is far more restricted than is the case with those belonging to the Aurignacian culture. Solutrean man does not seem to have penetrated beyond the Pyrenees, except at their extreme eastern end, where a trickle down the east coast of the Spanish Peninsula as far as Valencia seems to have taken place. Solutrean industries are not found on the Riviera nor in Italy; indeed, no true Solutrean culture is found south of the Alps. In England a number of laurel leaves have been unearthed from open sites in the south-east of the country, and at least a Solutrean influence penetrated as far west as Kent's Cavern, Torquay, and as far north as Creswell Crags in Derbyshire. Many of the industries in central Europe were formerly considered to be Solutrean, but an examination of them indicates that they belong rather to an upper Aurignacian culture with a slight Solutrean admixture. In northern Hungary, however, as has already been said, rich early Solutrean finds abound. Whether or no an actual evolution of these people took place in this region, perhaps as hybridisation between the Aurignacian culture and some aboriginal flake-tool culture of the district, or whether the Solutreans were really cradled somewhere still further to the east and merely occupied northern Hungary for a considerable period, is not known. Should the latter prove to be the case, the Solutreans might perhaps be considered somewhat in the light of a prehistoric Hunnish invasion of the west which succeeded, there being no Roman legions to stop their advance at Châlons!

The Solutrean culture in western Europe can be dated to a time when the second maximum of the last glaciation, Würm II, was approaching.

Before leaving the Solutrean culture, a word of warning must be given to the student. Laurel leaves have a much wider distribution than those of the true Solutrean culture and they are not necessarily indicative of it. It seems to be a fact, perhaps difficult to explain, that contact between a Neanthropic culture and one belonging to the flake-tool civilisation leads to the development of the laurel leaf tool type. This is true in South Africa and in Kenya and in many other regions. As has been said, it may also be true in northern Hungary of the Solutrean culture itself. In the literature the word "Solutrean" is somewhat loosely used: properly speaking, it should of course mean that the Solutrean culture itself is present. As, however, the laurel leaf was formerly considered to be a typical Solutrean tool, it sometimes happens that when it is found the word "Solutrean" is applied to the whole

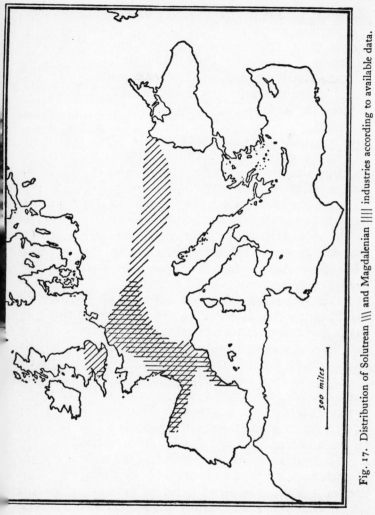

Fig. 17. Distribution of Solutrean \\\ and Magdalenian ||||| industries according to available data.

500 miles

industry. This is of course an incorrect use of the term and until new evidence is forthcoming no serious penetration of the true Solutrean culture into such areas as the Spanish Peninsula,[1] Italy, Palestine, etc., can be admitted. Furthermore, it is incorrect on the evidence of laurel leaves to affirm that Solutrean man himself ever entered the African Continent.

THE MAGDALENIAN CULTURE. In areas where the Solutreans never penetrated, the Aurignacian culture continued to develop independently, and as a result we find a series of industries Solutrean in date, but late Aurignacian in character. In France this development, perhaps influenced by the Solutrean invaders, gave rise to the Magdalenian culture which has given us the marvellous works of art belonging to the so-called "Reindeer Age"—for this was, *par excellence*, the period of palaeolithic artistic activity.

A six-fold subdivision has been found possible for the Magdalenian culture. In the industries belonging to the first three of these, no trace of any form of harpoon has been discovered and the subdivisions are largely characterised by different kinds of bone lance points (Fig. 9, 5 and 7). Magdalenian (4) yields the primitive harpoon, Magdalenian (5) the harpoon with the single row of barbs (Fig. 9, *11*), and Magdalenian (6) the two varieties of harpoon with a double row of barbs (p. 80 and Fig. 9, 9 and 2). To some extent, too, the different subdivisions are typified by the different kinds of patterns used for decorating the bone weapons. This matter will be considered again in the chapter on the home art. While beautifully made scrapers, gravers,

1 Except, as has been said, for a few finds north of the Cordillera Cantabrica and down the east coast. But here the well-made tanged arrow-heads may owe their origin to the Aterian of North Africa rather than to the true Solutrean.

awls, etc., occur in the Magdalenian industries, mostly made on blades, as a whole other materials such as bone, horn, antler and ivory, were especially used by these people for tool-making purposes, and a very high degree of skill was attained in their production, though at the end of the period a distinct degeneration in the industries set in.

Skeletons of this date are not uncommon and in type recall those of Cro-Magnon. Careful or ceremonial burial was frequently practised; red ochre being much in evidence and the bodies being decorated with shell necklaces. Indeed, in some cases they were actually almost buried in shells. One of the best known finds of human remains was that made at Chancelade in the Dordogne, and attempts have been made to correlate this skeleton anatomically with that of certain Eskimo. The sort of life lived by the Eskimo to-day must have been somewhat similar to that lived by Magdalenian man. The climate was still arctic in its rigour, although varying slightly at different moments during the Magdalenian period. At one time at any rate reindeer actually penetrated as far south as Mentone! On the whole it was somewhat damper than in Solutrean times, for whereas then cold dry steppe conditions prevailed and such animals as the saïga antelope were common, throughout the Magdalenian period, especially in its middle phases, the steppe conditions were less rigorous and reindeer abounded; though, if the representations of that animal made by Magdalenian man himself can be taken into account, it was in western France rather of a forest type, while in the east of the country, close under the Alpine ice, the tundra form existed.

It cannot be too strongly urged on the student that the Magdalenian culture proper seems to be a French development and that strictly speaking it is only found very sporadically outside France and Spain north of the Cordillera Cantabrica. It is true that its influence seems to have spread somewhat further, and very occasionally isolated Magdalenian tools have been found elsewhere, but these do not occur in a Magdalenian milieu but with an industry that is essentially a development of the late Aurignacian which, as has been said, continued to evolve throughout Solutrean times in areas where Solutrean man did not settle. Even at Mentone no Solutrean or Magdalenian industries have been found but thick Aurignacian deposits occur, and a study of the fauna in the upper layers demonstrates that these are contemporary with the Magdalenian culture of France. The same is true in Moravia. Unfortunately, no satisfactory name has yet been devised for this late development of the Aurignacian culture contemporary with that of the Solutreans and Magdalenians elsewhere. Locally in England it is often called "Creswellian" after the well-known sites at Creswell Crags on the borders of Nottinghamshire and Derbyshire which were meticulously excavated by A. L. Armstrong. Here the contemporaneity of the latest Aurignacian industry with the Magdalenian of France is further demonstrated by the occurrence of one undoubted Magdalenian decorated bone lance point among the developed Aurignacian implements. It is true that the Magdalenians, like their Solutrean forbears, just trickled down the eastern coastline of the Spanish Peninsula, and it seems possible in view of the occurrence of cave art at La Pileta and at one or two other sites in the province of Malaga that they actually penetrated in this way as far as the south-west of the Peninsula. But their industries are not found inland, nor do they occur in

Italy, Palestine or central Europe; and as far as our own country is concerned they do not seem to have penetrated except perhaps in the extreme south-west where certain finds at Kent's Cavern, Cheddar and Aveline's Hole (Mendip) may perhaps be assigned to a true though late Magdalenian culture.

Deposits containing certain Magdalenian industries have been found in eastern France resting on moraines belonging to the last glaciation (Würm I). As the climate during Magdalenian times was both cold and somewhat damper than during late Aurignacian and Solutrean periods, it is usual to correlate this culture with Würm II (Bühl) and it is probable that the latest Magdalenian came just after this cold oscillation.

Right at the end of Magdalenian times the industries in south France underwent a change which appears in the Pyrenees first and later in the Dordogne. Round scrapers, curved knife blades (Fig. 5, 5) and the parrot beak type of graver (Fig. 4, 8) appear, as well as large pyramidal core-scrapers and core-gravers (Fig. 4, 11); small shoulder-points, too, can be noted although very different in form from their Aurignacian forerunners. The bone industry becomes poorer; engravings in the home art become less vigorous and more mechanical; conventionalisation increases, new influences are being brought to bear on the Magdalenian world. All this coincides with a rapid change of climate which was taking place and this change heralds the end of quaternary times and shuts the book on the last of the cultures of the Old Stone Age.

Chapter X

THE HOME ART

WHEN excavating an upper palaeolithic home site in the mouth of a cave or rock-shelter, one frequently comes across bone tools, portions of which have been carved into the shapes of animals' heads or have had their surfaces covered with engravings of animals or signs or patterns: often too there are fragments of bone or suitable pieces of stone that are similarly engraved. Not only is it astonishing that such manifestations of artistic activity should occur at such an early date, but it is doubly amazing to observe to what a high degree of proficiency these upper palaeolithic artists had already attained. It is safe to say that there is not one person in a thousand in this country to-day who would be capable even after some drawing lessons of emulating the works of art that were made by these old folk so many thousands of years ago.

French prehistorians have given the inclusive name of "*art mobilier*" to these various carved or decorated objects which are found in the prehistoric homes. For this expression there is no exact English translation but, since it is essentially in the home sites rather than the cave interiors that the objects occur, it does not seem improper to use the term "home art".

Theoretically there is no reason why examples of the home art should not also be found in open stations of upper palaeolithic date. Indeed, engravings have been brought forward, but unfortunately in every case so far there has been, for various reasons, an element of doubt as to the authenticity or the true age of the specimen. In the nature of the case it would be hardly likely that such fragile objects as decorated bones, etc., would often survive the rough and tumble and mechanical weathering to which industries from open stations are almost invariably exposed.[1]

When we come to examine the home art of cave-mouth or rock-shelter sites, however, problems of authenticity and dating of specimens seldom prove a difficulty, for they are constantly found associated with datable industries, often in sealed deposits, and we can therefore confidently assert that they were the work of artists belonging to particular cultures.

✓Comprising the home art there are paintings, engravings, cut bone silhouettes, carved reliefs, both high and low and sculptured objects.

As might be expected, paintings have rarely been preserved. Even when the pigment used was such a

[1] At this point a word of warning must be given to the student in respect to so-called "figure stones". These consist of natural pieces of flint that appear—when held up the right way—to resemble some natural object such as an animal's head. Flint often assumes somewhat grotesque shapes and such chance resemblances are by no means rare. Before deciding that mankind has had any hand in the shaping of such specimens, it is of course necessary to be sure that definite human working has been done on the object. Invariably it will be found that such evidence is lacking and that the specimen is merely a *lusus naturae*. Of course it can always be argued that prehistoric man observed the chance likeness and therefore collected the specimen, and, especially when a *lusus naturae* occurs associated with a definite human industry, such a belief is not unreasonable. But it seems doubtful whether this explanation is often satisfactory and in the vast majority of cases no such association can be demonstrated. Such "figure stones", however, have somehow or other attracted the attention of a number of people who seem to become fascinated by them and who are most unwilling to admit that they are simply and solely the result of nature's handiwork.

substance as red ochre, of a nature as permanent as rock itself, the slight mechanical weathering which must have taken place in the deposits, as well as the considerable surface decay to which such a rock as limestone—a not unusual canvas of the home artists— is liable as a result of the chemical action of humic acids, etc., would tend to ensure their destruction in practically every instance. It is surprising that any have survived at all rather than that such survivals are so few and far between. Of any paintings which may have been made with more fugitive colouring matters, such as powdered burnt bones, naturally hardly a trace has remained until to-day. However, we have been fortunate at a site near Sergeac in the Dordogne, where a very good painting of a stag, of Aurignacian date, has been unearthed (Fig. 19, 7), as well as other figures, including a bichrome one, of the same date. From Laugerie Basse, near Les Eyzies, come portions of a painted bison of Magdalenian age, but these and a few other examples of less importance are practically all we have to show in the way of paintings in the home art. Some of the small ivory statuettes representing women may possibly have also been originally painted, as it would appear that minute traces of red ochre still adhere in their interstices. But how far this was in any sense a general rule we cannot now say. On the other hand innumerable engravings—on fragments of bone, on suitable pieces of stone and on fashioned bone tools—have been found. The style of the drawings is by no means always the same and many of them are beautifully executed.

In the past it has been taken as axiomatic that the production of sculpture must necessarily have preceded that of line engraving: that people desirous of representing natural objects would start by making models in the round and only later discover the possibilities of line drawing. This theory was based on the psychological belief that primitive man would have a certain difficulty in comprehending a representation made in only two dimensions, and that therefore three dimensional representations of three dimensional objects must have been first practised. Be this as it may, and the argument seems to me to be open to dispute, the facts are that engravings do occur from the very beginning. Their numbers, however, compared with those of the sculptured objects are at first relatively very small and this proportion steadily increases until, at the end of upper palaeolithic times, it is reversed and engravings are far more abundant than sculptures.

Bone silhouettes are not found before Magdalenian times. They consist of thin flat pieces of bone cut into the shapes of animals. They are not true sculptures, of course, but they were often very skilfully made and, as far as the thinness of the material would allow, were beautifully finished off with engraved additions of eyes, etc. A painter's palette from the Grotte de Rey, near Les Eyzies, cut into the form of a fish comes at once to one's mind, a really delightful object (Fig. 18, 5). Both high and low relief carvings in stone are sometimes found in the home art. As examples one can cite the woman carrying a bison's horn (Fig. 18, 1), as well as other similar figures cut on blocks of limestone, which were found in late Aurignacian deposits at Laussel, a few miles from Les Eyzies. Though cumbersome objects and difficult to move about, these are generally classed with the home art as they were actually unearthed in a home site. The fact that they originally perhaps formed part of a frieze decorating the wall of the rock-shelter home which subsequently fell into and became incorporated in the deposits below seems no adequate reason for excluding them.

True sculptures are frequent and especially note-worthy are the "Venuses" (Plate IV) which have been already mentioned in another connection when the origin of the upper palaeolithic cultures of western Europe was under consideration. There are also a fair number of small beautifully made sculptures of animals such as the well-known horse from the Grotte de la Madeleine at Lourdes.

It is somewhat usual to-day to spell art with a capital A, thus personifying and giving it a separate existence independent of the particular people or culture responsible for its production. This is of course an unfortunate habit, the result of loose thinking. Art is an expression of culture, expressing perhaps the genius of that culture but necessarily showing a parallel develop-ment or evolutionary cycle. Of course the artistic ideas of neighbouring cultures, whether ancient or modern, must influence each other in varying degrees, but essen-tially it is impossible to separate them from the culture-soil in which they are rooted. Thus it is inaccurate to talk of "upper palaeolithic art" and treat it as a single whole independent of the various cultures which pro-duced it. We shall therefore proceed to discuss the home art of upper palaeolithic times under the three headings: Aurignacian, Solutrean and Madgalenian.

AURIGNACIAN HOME ART. Certain rare Aurignacian paintings have already been mentioned as well as the occurrence of sculptured "Venuses". These latter (Plate IV) represent women, frequently apparently pregnant; in many cases they were probably connected with some

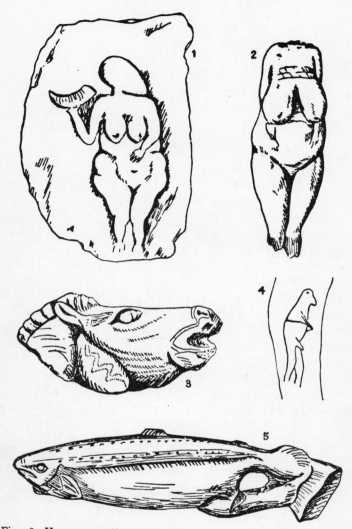

Fig. 18. Home art. 1, Venus of Laussel. 2, Venus of Kostenki. 3, Horse's head from Mas d'Azil. 4, Engraving on bone from Creswell Crags. 5, Fish palette from the Grotte de Rey.

fertility cult. As we have seen, they are important
evidence of the partial Asiatic origin of the Aurignacian
culture in western Europe. One of the most important
sites in south-western France which has yielded such
sculpture is at Brassempouy, in the Landes district not
far from Orthez. Two cave-homes have been explored—
the Grotte du Pape and the Grotte des Hyènes—and rich
Aurignacian and Solutrean finds made. The statuettes
are made of mammoth ivory and are, it would seem,
of fairly early Aurignacian date (Fig. 19, 4). Further
eastwards, in the Haute Garonne at Lespugue, a very
peculiar statuette was discovered showing a conventional treatment; the features are not differentiated and
the footless legs are fused together and taper to a point;
the breasts are also placed extremely low on the body
and the position of the head and neck is schematic (Plate
IV, 1). The caves near Mentone have also yielded one or
two of these figurines. In central Europe at Willendorf,
a loess site on the left bank of the Danube, a few miles
below Melk in Austria, two statuettes have been discovered. One of these is the famous "Venus of Willendorf" (Plate IV, 2). It is a grotesque female figure some
4½ inches high made of fine grained oolitic limestone.
The legs are short and squat, the breasts and abdomen
extremely exaggerated, the head is bent and elaborately
coiffured, no facial features having been attempted.
Very considerable development of the buttocks and
hips are indicated. But the arms are almost non-
existent so faintly are they shown; they are in fact
bent at the elbows, the hands resting on the breasts.
Some distance further to the north-east at a loess site
near Unter Wisternitz in Moravia, a few miles south
of Brno, there has been found another Venus (Plate
IV, 3) somewhat more discreetly treated than the one at

Willendorf. At both sites rich Aurignacian industries, seemingly rather late in date, occur. In Italy, at Savignano sul Panàro in the Apennines of Emilia, there has been discovered a female statuette considerably conventionalised although showing something of the characteristic features seen on other Aurignacian examples. The head is absent but the development of the breasts, abdomen and buttocks is very considerable and, as so often is the case, the legs are fused together and end in a point. The object is sculptured in serpentine and is green in colour. Unfortunately we have no stratigraphical information in connection with this find as it was discovered accidentally by workmen. As we go eastwards the number of statuettes discovered tends to increase; the famous example from Kostenki (Fig. 18, 2), in the middle of Russia, may be instanced together with other numerous examples, often treated in a very conventional manner, which have been found at Malta, not far from Lake Baikal (Fig. 19, 2). This list includes the more notable finds of these extremely important female statuettes; others have been found, for instance a large number come from the valley of the Don in Russia, but it is not necessary to enumerate them all here.

Besides these Aurignacian sculptures and the reliefs such as the Venus of Laussel (Fig. 18, 1) already mentioned, there are also a number of engravings, some of early Aurignacian date, such as the engraving of the hind-quarters of a horse (Fig. 19, 6) found on a piece of bone in the deposits at Hornos de la Peña, north Spain, others, of late Aurignacian date, as for example the very beautiful engravings of horses, etc., which were found at Labatut, near Sergeac, in the Dordogne (Fig. 19, 5). It is interesting to observe the evolution in technique from the earlier simple outline engravings such as the Hornos de la Peña horse to the far more skilfully drawn figures from Labatut. From Le Trilobite, a site near Arcy-sur-Cure, Yonne, comes among other things an engraving of early Aurignacian date depicting a rhinoceros. Such animals were rarely figured in upper palaeolithic art and therefore this example is worthy of note.[1]

In Moravia, besides the female sculptures, we have also other specimens of home art. These appear to belong to the late Aurignacian date rather than to the Solutrean culture, to which it has been usual in the past to assign them. While normal sculptures occur, such as that of a little mammoth found at Unter Wisternitz, there are also examples showing a peculiar method of treatment. Especially important in this respect is the well-known site of Předmost in Moravia which has yielded two famous figures representing a mammoth and a woman. Both are treated in a very conventionalised manner, the former being sculptured in the round. Too thick to be described as a bone silhouette it is too thin for true sculpture, and the whole is covered with a series of fine engraved lines. The female figure, engraved on ivory, is geometrically conventionalised (Fig. 19, 3) in a manner which only an illustration can convey. The exact connection between this rather peculiar central European style of art and that of the west has not yet been completely determined. It brings to mind, however, certain very peculiar late palaeolithic art manifestations in Russia, for example, the finds from the Rue St Cyril at Kiev, and those at Mézine. But a detailed investigation of this rather specialised and as yet not fully studied branch of the subject would obviously be out of place in the present volume.

[1] A simple engraving of a man was found at Cresswell Crags. Fig. 18, 4.

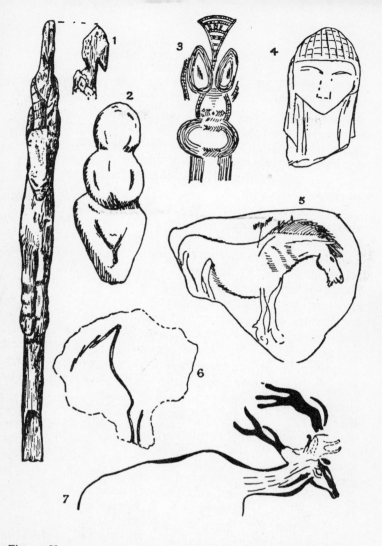

Fig. 19. Home art. 1, Carved ibex spear-thrower. 2, Sketch of a Venus from Malta, Siberia. 3, Engraved Venus from Předmost. 4, Venus of Brassempouy. 5, Late Aurignacian engraving from Labatut, Sergeac. 6, Early Aurignacian engraving from Hornos de la Peña. 7, Aurignacian painting from Sergeac.

SOLUTREAN HOME ART. It used to be thought that the Solutreans were completely inartistic and that no art of Solutrean date existed. Later, when some reliefs undoubtedly belonging to this period were unearthed, it was suggested that they were the product of the aboriginal Aurignacians over whom the Solutrean invaders dominated as a ruling caste. This suggestion may have some truth in it, but the number of Solutrean art finds has gradually increased, and not only have reliefs representing animals been discovered at the cave of Isturitz, Basses-Pyrénées and at Le Roc, Charente (Plate V, 2) and other sites, but also undoubted engravings on stone have been discovered near Bourdeilles, a village on the banks of the Dronne about 16 miles to the north-west of Périgueux.[1] It has become therefore necessary to revise somewhat the old theories and to consider that, while the production of the art of this date may be largely due to the Aurignacian aboriginals, the Solutreans themselves, even if not its originators, were probably at any rate not antagonistic to its production. The find at Le Roc consisted of part of a circle composed of large blocks of stone on which animals had been carved in high relief. In one instance there is a scene apparently representing a man facing a musk ox. Among other animals figured are one or more examples of reindeer, oxen, birds (rarely depicted at all in palaeolithic art), ibex, bison, etc. The whole is very impressive.

No true sculptures associated with Solutrean industries and of undoubted Solutrean age have yet been discovered.

[1] Archives de l'Inst. de Pal. Hum. Mem. 10, by D. Peyrony.

MAGDALENIAN HOME ART. The skill displayed by the Magdalenians in their artistic productions is indeed impressive. Marvellous as are the results achieved in the Aurignacian and Solutrean art cycles, very few of them show much real artistic merit even when they give us a sense of vigour and power and amaze us on account of their great antiquity. But when we come to look at the achievements of Magdalenian man we are frequently astounded not only at the skill displayed by the artists, but also at the genuine beauty of many of their productions. Take, for instance, the little sculpture representing a horse's head found at Mas d'Azil (Fig. 18, 3); this would be a glorious object to possess, quite apart from any considerations as to its age. Or, again, consider the reindeer turning its head figured on Plate VI.[1] Such objects are a continual source of joy to the beholder and examples of them can be multiplied many times over. As has been already stated, the Magdalenian period has been divided into six stages. Attempts have been made, with not a little success, to correlate certain peculiar styles often noticeable in the Magdalenian home art with these different subdivisions. Especially has this been found possible when the geometric patterns which are frequently engraved on Magdalenian objects are studied. Fig. 20 illustrates a few of the more characteristic ones. Geometric patterns as a source of decoration are usually of a simple order: zigzags, straight lines with little dots at intervals, spirals, and combinations of these, are about the most complicated motifs that we find. Such patterns, as well as the methods of treatment of the naturalistic animal figures, varied from time to time, very much as fashion varies to-day.

[1] This object is in the author's private collection.

In levels of Magdalenian (1) and (2) date there have been found not a few *bâtons de commandment*, the extremities of which had been sculptured into the forms of animal heads. In Magdalenian (3) levels, besides

engravings of animals which are sometimes executed *en pointillé*, the spiral motif appears as well as zigzags broken by transverse lines. In Magdalenian (4) levels we often find the association of sculpture with engraving, an attempt being made to give a sense of relief to the figures. Magdalenian (5) is the period of the best engravings, though no longer is any attempt at indicating relief made. Many of the drawings, such as the reindeer on Plate VI, are really beautiful. During the period covered by Magdalenian (6) degeneration began to set in, the engravings became somewhat deeper and more mechanically made, e.g. the horse's head from Laugerie Basse (Plate VI). They no longer show the triumphs of skill of the earlier period.

Besides more or less naturalistic representations of animals and geometric patterns there is found in the Magdalenian art cycle a considerable number of what may be called suggestion pictures which show only the one or more salient features of a naturalistic figure or figures, the rest being suppressed. For convenience we may perhaps divide these into two groups: the one, suggestion pictures, the other, simple conventionalisations of a single subject. As an example of the first we may take the engravings on a small bone found at Teyjat in the Dordogne (Fig. 20). Here the artist has wished to depict a herd of reindeer. He has drawn with some degree of skill the three foremost and the last animals, while in the middle he has indicated a forest of antlers. The whole sketch is only a few inches long yet the impression of the presence of a vast herd of beasts is admirably given. This shows artistic technique of a very high order. In the second case, the figure of a single animal is taken and reduced to its simplest terms, certain outstanding characteristics being selected. For example, let us consider a horse's head seen full face. One notes the length of the head, the presence of two ears, and projecting between them the mane. In its simplest form, then, a horse's head can be represented by a trident, the middle fork of the prongs being shorter than the other two. A conventionalisation of an ox, on the other hand, will show no mane, but besides the two ears there will be also two horns, and the final result will be a straight line from the top of which branch obliquely four shorter lines, two to the right and two to the left, respectively. Naturally an observer happening to meet with one of these completely conventionalised figures frequently cannot explain what they were meant to represent, and it is only with careful study and after collecting all the intervening links in the chain from the naturalistic representation to the completely conventionalised one—i.e. when the complete series has been obtained—that one can say definitely what these conventionalisations were intended to mean. A detailed study of this matter unfortunately is hardly within the province of this book and moreover the problem has not yet been completely elucidated. One interesting point, however, might be

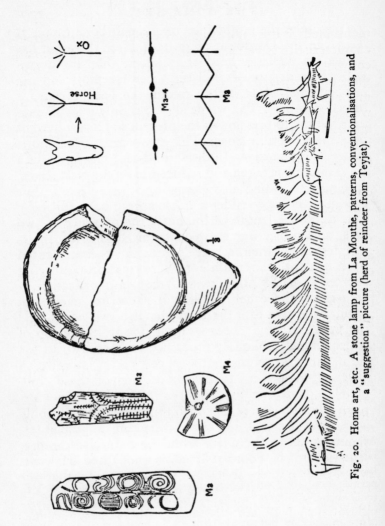

Fig. 20. Home art, etc. A stone lamp from La Mouthe, patterns, conventionalisations, and a "suggestion" picture (herd of reindeer from Teyjat).

mentioned: it does not necessarily follow that the same characteristics have been selected every time. The final conventionalisations of a given natural object will not then be necessarily exactly similar in all cases. There may occur, thus, two apparently totally different figures whose connection can only be understood when the original naturalistic figure from which they are derived is known. Conventionalisations appear with ever greater frequency towards the end of Magdalenian times. Indeed, they seem to be a product of an overripe civilisation and they herald the beginning of the end. The best period—the period of greatest vigour—coincides with the most beautiful naturalistic representations, and only afterwards do conventionalisations appear in greater and greater numbers. The first kind of suggestion pictures may perhaps be exempted from this stricture: they after all represent an attempt to indicate a whole scene which clearly is too large to be put on the small canvas available. They are in a different category from the conventionalisations of single animals, some of them may, indeed, have been meant to convey a message—an idea which makes us think about the earliest beginnings of writing.

ADDENDUM. An important site, in process of exploration by Dr Garrod and her colleagues, is situated near the village of Angles-sur-l'Anglin (Vienne) and is called the Roc aux Sorciers. Mousterian tools have for a long time been known from this large rock-shelter. Recently Magdalenian III and VI levels have been discovered. Belonging to the earlier Magdalenian period and buried under deposits containing Magdalenian VI tools occur sculptured reliefs on the walls of the shelter. They include bison, horse and representations of women from the waist downwards. There is also a group of five ibex, and, on a limestone block, a man's head which has also been partly painted and engraved. The final publication of these finds will add much to our knowledge of early Magdalenian art.

Chapter XI

THE CAVE ART

EVEN more interesting than the works of art found in the prehistoric homes are a number of paintings and engravings which adorn the walls of caves in various parts of southern France and Spain. These caves were not inhabited in their depths and, as we shall see later on, they were probably used as cult shrines. The drawings include figures of animals of various kinds, human beings (very rare), human hands and a number of signs which can best be realised by reference to Fig. 27, and are generally called tectiforms.

To begin with, a word or two as to the distribution of the cave art is necessary. Obviously there can be no cave art where there are no caves, and suitable caves are only found in limestone districts. It follows, then, that only in localities where limestone occurs can we expect to find these paintings and engravings. Districts in France and Spain where the conditions are satisfactory and where indeed we do find the cave art occur in the departments of the Dordogne, Corrèze, Ariège, Haute Garonne, Gard, and Ardèche; and, in northern Spain, in the provinces of Cantabria and Asturias, that is to say, westwards of Bilbao[1] from the Pass of Carranza along the southern coast of the Bay of Biscay north of the watershed of the Cordillera Cantabrica.[2] In such

[1] The painted cave of Santimamiñe (Basondo: Cortézubi) has been found, however, just to the east of Bilbao.

[2] One or two unimportant sites are actually known just south of the mountain massif, but they are undoubtedly part of the northern complex.

an intervening district as the Landes of France doubtless similar art-loving tribes existed, but they could
never have drawn on the walls of caves even if they had
wanted to for the simple reason that no caves existed
in their country. No evidence, then, as to the distribution of the upper palaeolithic artists can be hoped for
from a mere study of the distribution of the cave art
alone. In south Spain, a small anomalous group of
painted caves has been found in the province of Malaga
eastwards from Gibraltar. How the artists got there
and what was their connection with their brother crafts-
men north of the Pyrenees and Cordillera Cantabrica is
still a problem. Outside these districts but little cave art
has been found, except at a site near Palermo in Sicily
and in Levanzo, an island off the west coast. At Grotta
Romanelli, a cave in the heel of Italy, both wall engravings and Aurignacian industries occur. So there is
no reason to refuse a similar date for the engravings.
The rock-shelter art of eastern Spain (see Chapter XIII),
though in part late palaeolithic, is quite distinct. On the
whole, however, it can be affirmed with a fair degree
of certainty that this cave art is confined almost exclusively to the extreme west of Europe. Unfortunately,
none has yet been discovered in England.

The question of how the engravings and paintings
were made must next be considered. That the engravings
were undoubtedly made with burins there is direct
evidence at the Trois Frères, a cave in the Pyrenees,
where, on the left-hand wall of a small alcove leading
off from one of the passages, the first explorer discovered a flint graver resting on a small projecting knob
of wall just below a very fine engraving of a lion. It
seems highly probable that the artist after making the
picture had left the tool on this handy natural pro-

jection, and that there it had remained until it was discovered thousands of years afterwards.

As regards the paintings, various kinds of pigments were collected and used by upper palaeolithic man, naturally occurring ochres being especially useful for his purpose. We have already seen that red ochre was used in ceremonial burials, and it is not unlikely that this colouring matter was also used for painting the living body. Ochres commonly occur naturally and little heaps of this material collected by man are often found in the homes. In composition ochres are oxides of iron mixed, more or less, with earth and clayey impurities. In colour they vary from chocolate to light red and from orange to yellow. In the former case they may be called varieties of haematite, in the latter of limonite. The colours are absolutely permanent, as lasting as that of rock itself. Besides ochres another naturally occurring mineral ore, oxide of manganese, was sometimes used. This, when powdered, gives a blue-black pigment. A coal black was obtained from burnt bones, but this substance, composed as it is of carbon, is somewhat fugitive and liable to oxidation. No other substance seems to have been utilised by upper palaeolithic man unless, indeed, he used some vegetable preparations which have now completely disappeared. The paintings, then, are in shades of red, yellow and black, no true blues, greens or white ever occurring. The pigment seems to have been ground up into a fine powder, and kept in little tubes made of hollow bones stopped up at one end, examples of which have actually been found. It was then mixed with some fatty substance, easily obtained from the animals that were hunted and killed for food, and the resulting paint applied to the cave wall. How the application was made we do not

PLATE VI

Engravings of a reindeer turning its head, and a horse,
both from Laugerie Basse.

know. There is no reason, however, to deny the possibility that some form of paint-brush was employed. Such paint-brushes could have been easily manufactured —the animals at the period were mostly hairy or furry on account of the cold climate, and it would not have been difficult to obtain the necessary materials. In some instances, however, small stamps[1] were used, and especially was this the case where the outline of an animal was formed by a series of punctuations (see p. 192) as these themselves often show a distinct shape such as would result from the use of a small stamp dipped in the paint and then pressed on to the cave wall.

The fact that the pigments seem to have been mixed with fat has led to some curious results. Limestone is somewhat porous and rain falling on the surface of a hill slowly percolates through minute pores and fissures in the rock, emerging in the caves as a slow dripping from the roof or a sweating of the walls. Either such a sweating erodes the surface of the wall or, in certain circumstances, a thin film of stalactite (calcium carbonate) may be deposited. This happens when the percolating water is charged with carbonic acid, thus enabling a strong solution of calcium bicarbonate to be formed, from which the normal (insoluble) carbonate gets precipitated on the cave wall when its carbon dioxide is given off. Thus where a sweating of the wall has taken place either the surface will be slightly etched away or there may be an actual deposit of stalactite. When, however, the minute pores in the limestone have become clogged with the fatty material no sweating of the walls takes place and as a result

[1] Doubtless made of some soft substance such as wood, perhaps covered with a bit of skin.

neither erosion of the surface of the wall can there take place nor any deposition of stalactite upon it.

There is a very good instance of this curious and interesting phenomenon at Niaux near Tarascon-en-Ariège. A whole panel of rock-surface has become considerably etched except where the painted outline of an animal occurs. This painted outline has remained smooth, but the charcoal that was originally used as the colouring matter has oxidised away. To-day, then, there appears an eroded surface of wall on which can be seen in certain lights a smooth outline of an animal in silver grey standing out in slight relief. If deposition of stalactite had taken place rather than an etching of the wall, the figure would of course have been in low instead of high relief. Naturally, where very much percolation has taken place no amount of painting has prevented wall sweating, and much destruction of the drawings, either complete or partial, has undoubtedly taken place. But in the case of a good compact material such as carboniferous limestone percolation is slow and does not by any means take place everywhere, so that good fortune has preserved for us either wholly or in part a large number of these wonderful manifestations of the artistic activity of upper palaeolithic man.

Most of the paintings are found at considerable distances from the entrances of the caves and often deep in the interior of the hillsides far removed from daylight; and even in the case of such a site as Marsoulas, where to-day they are found not far from the entrance, it would seem probable that originally the cave extended further along the hill-side than it now does, and that its entrance was further from them than is now the case. Some form of artificial light, then, must have been used by upper palaeolithic man both when he wished to make or visit the drawings. This matter is not quite so simple as it might appear at first sight. At the cave of Niaux, for example, the paintings are found near the centre of the hill, something like half a mile from the entrance, and to visit them to-day it is necessary to use large miners' acetylene lamps. Of course with the help of a candle or two one can stumble along, but care has to be taken that the source of illumination will last for several hours and that one has means of re-lighting should an accidental drop of water falling from the roof or any other cause extinguish the light. It is therefore not simply a case of seizing a burning brand from the fire and with this alone visiting the painted cave: there must have been proper lamps. Lamps made of stone have, indeed, been discovered. A very well-made example with the engraving of an ibex on the bottom, containing in it when found a certain amount of carbonaceous matter, has been discovered at La Mouthe, near Les Eyzies in the Dordogne (Fig. 20). More generally, however, it would seem likely that some skull of an animal was used for the purpose. The fuel was probably some sort of fat or marrow and the wick some kind of moss. Such a lamp was probably not unlike those used by the Eskimo to-day. The illumination must have been poor but would have been steady and constant, and would have lasted for a considerable period.

AUTHENTICITY. The authenticity of the cave art, unlike that of the home art, has had to be demonstrated. Many of the caves have remained open ever since palaeolithic times and it thus becomes necessary to prove: (i) that the art is really upper palaeolithic in date and not the work of some later people in historical times, and

(ii) that the cave art is not the work of modern forgers. For this purpose let us visit in imagination certain sites and observe any relevant evidence. We shall start with the small cave of Pair-non-Pair on the right bank of the Dordogne just before it joins the Garonne to form the Gironde. When first discovered, this consisted of a small rock-shelter into which one could penetrate on one's hands and knees for but a short distance. In the soil were found flint implements and a local prehistorian (M. Daleau) decided to excavate the site. This was done with meticulous care during twenty years, the position of every object found being carefully recorded. An upper Aurignacian industry with Gravette knife blades and also some proto-Solutrean tools was found. Below this came a level containing middle Aurignacian tools such as keeled scrapers and beaked gravers, etc. Below this again was discovered a lower Aurignacian level with Châtelperron points, and yet lower still a typical Mousterian industry with side-scrapers and points. Last of all at the base there was another Mousterian or perhaps Acheulean layer. As the excavation continued, the floor level of the cave was lowered and the site was found to consist of a deep narrow fissure penetrating some little distance into the hill, and when bed-rock was reached an ancient entrance below that known at the start of the work was unmasked. As the floor-level was lowered by the excavations and the walls of the fissure exposed, these were found to be covered with engravings. Now it is obvious that these engravings cannot be of later date than the deposits which covered them in and these actually contained upper Aurignacian implements. This proof alone is sufficient to demonstrate the existence of engravings in Aurignacian times.

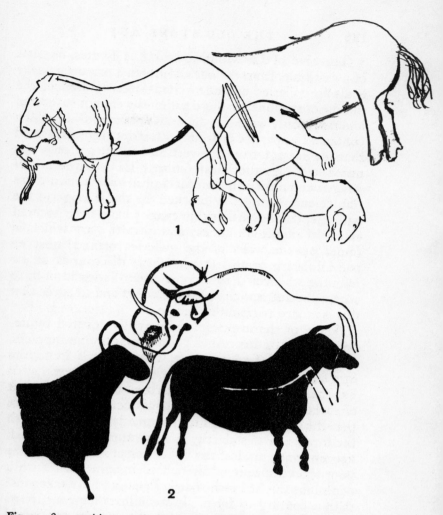

Fig. 21. Superpositions. 1, At Teyjat, superpositions of engravings of the same phase (phase C) and style. 2, At Font-de-Gaume, superpositions of paintings of different phases—the head of a rhinoceros in red outline (phase A), covered by a black outline figure (probably phase B) which also overlies an ox in flat-wash (phase C). A slightly polychrome bison (phase D) overlies another phase C ox as well as the phase A rhino and the phase B figure.

The cave of La Mouthe, near Les Eyzies, consists of a vestibule, from the back of which a narrow passage leads to galleries behind. When first explored in the middle of the nineties these galleries were not suspected and it was only when the deposits in the vestibule which contained upper palaeolithic industries were excavated that the passage from the vestibule to the galleries was unmasked. As the latest finds at La Mouthe are of Magdalenian date and as the deposits containing these implements completely blocked up the passage to the galleries, it follows that this cannot have been entered since Magdalenian times, and that the art which is found on the walls of the galleries behind must be palaeolithic in date. It was these discoveries at La Mouthe which first forced the scientific world both to accept the authenticity of the cave art and to agree that it was indeed palaeolithic in age.

Many of the drawings are partially covered by deposits of stalactite. As a good example one may cite an engraving of an animal at Hornos de la Peña, the fore and hind quarters of which are completely visible but the middle of which is obscured by a thick deposit of carbonate of lime. Careful scratching demonstrates that the engraving runs under this deposit. Although the formation of stalactite is very capricious, and thick deposits may under certain circumstances form in a very short time, it is difficult to imagine that such a deposit as this at Hornos de la Peña can have taken less than a century to form. It sometimes happens, however, that figures of animals extinct from the world altogether are partially covered by such a formation of stalactite, and a century or so ago peasants living in remote valleys in northern Spain or southern France could never have heard of the existence of such extinct animals. These two facts then taken in conjunction demonstrate that we cannot be dealing with the work of modern forgers nor indeed with people living only a few centuries ago; they must be the work of artists who actually saw these extinct animals roaming about: in other words the art must date back to late pleistocene times.

Lastly, one may mention that at several sites (Bernifal near Les Eyzies, Gargas in the Pyrenees and Altamira in north Spain for instances) land slides have subsequently blocked up the entrances to the caves which have only been rediscovered in recent times. The story of Altamira may be taken as an example and this site is doubly interesting because it was here that the palaeolithic cave art was recognised for the first time. The cave opens on the downs not far from the little village of Santillana del Mar, some two and a half miles from Torrelavega, a town on the railway line from Santander to Madrid. It was discovered in the middle of the last century when digging out a fox that had run to earth, as the entrance had been completely masked by a small landslide. A short time afterwards a Spanish nobleman, the Marquis de Sautuola, and his small daughter aged five, visited the new cave, because the former thought it might be worth while to undertake a small excavation in the hope of finding the remains of prehistoric man. On entering the cave there is a vestibule full of rocks fallen from the roof, doubtless the remains of the landslide which blocked up the entrance. On the left, however, to-day behind a modern brick wall, there is a low chamber only a few feet high. It was here that the Marquis and his daughter decided to excavate. After a time the little girl, bored with her father's doings, took a candle and started walking about, and being

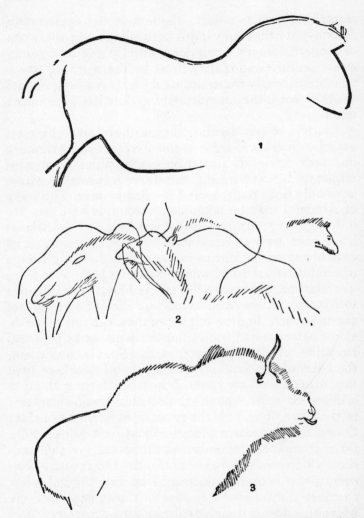

Fig. 22. Cave art engravings, phases A and B. 1, Horse at Hornos de la
Peña, phase A. 2, Figures at Gargas, phases A and B. 3, Bison close to
the throne at La Pasiéga, phase B.

small was able to stand upright and view the ceiling. Her cries of "Toro, Toro" attracted her father and the two of them for the first time for perhaps 10,000 years set eyes on the now famous painted ceiling where bison, horses, hinds, buck, boar, etc., are depicted, the animals being in some cases almost life size. What a moment it must have been for the father and his little girl! The results were duly published—and of course rejected by a sceptical scientific world. It was not until the excavations at La Mouthe demonstrated beyond doubt the age of the cave art that the previous discovery made by the Marquis and his daughter in 1879 was recalled.

STYLES AND PHASES. One of the first things that an explorer of a painted cave will notice is that the drawings are frequently made one on top of another, that there are superpositions or palimpsests. These are of great importance to the prehistorian, as naturally the law of superposition applies in the case of the drawings in exactly the same way as it does for deposits in the rock-shelters. Clearly a drawing on the top must be newer than that underneath it, which in turn must be newer than the one below it and so on.

Now when the engravings and paintings are critically studied it is found that they are not all by any means drawn in a similar manner. Various methods of depicting the three-dimensional animal on a two-dimensional "canvas" are employed. These are known as styles and it is significant to observe that while a certain number of these styles appear in the various districts where the cave art is found, they are by no means unlimited and the same ones can be observed in southern France and northern Spain. Such would hardly be the case if the art was the work of innumerable chance hunters who happened to wish to try their hands at drawing in the caves—but more of this in the next chapter. Certain styles can be grouped together into what—for the want of a better name—have been termed "phases". Whereas examples of styles within a phase are sometimes found drawn on top and sometimes under each other, the succession of the phases when in superposition is always constant (Fig. 21). It is believed that these phases are intimately connected with different cultures, and that therefore a definite sequence for the art can be determined. Four such phases can be observed and the following tables will show something of the work that has been done in this connection:

PHASE A

ENGRAVINGS

Simple outlines of animals made as if the shadow of the beast had been projected on the wall and a single line had then been drawn round it. At first only two legs are indicated and while the body of the animal is depicted in profile the head and horns are represented full-face. The eye is usually omitted and if present takes the form of a small oval. In the same period there occur meandering parallel lines, often called 'macaroni' which may have been primitive man's attempt at copying the scratches made by a cave bear when sharpening his claws on the cave wall. These latter are themselves frequently found. (Figs. 22, *1* and *2*, and 27 B).

PAINTINGS

Representations of the human hand either negative or positive. In the former case the hand is placed on the cave wall and the colour applied to the wall in such a way that when the hand is removed its representation appears uncoloured on a coloured background (Fig. 27 c). In the second case the hand itself is dipped in paint and stamped on the wall. Painted "macaroni" have occasionally been observed and simple outline drawings of animals corresponding to the engravings are found (Fig. 23, *1* and *2*).

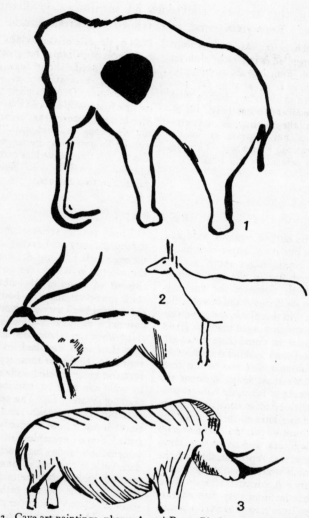

Fig. 23. Cave art paintings, phases A and B. 1, *Elephas antiquus* at Pindal, phase A. 2, Ibex and chamois at la Pasiéga, phases B and A respectively. 3, *Rhinoceros tichorhinus* at Font-de-Gaume, phase B.

PHASE B

ENGRAVINGS

Much better made engravings no longer showing only a single outline. Four legs are often represented and an attempt at perspective made when dealing with the head and horns (Fig. 22, *3*). Often the outline is not continuous but appears as in the illustration, Fig. 22, *3*. The eye, when present, is still oval.

PAINTINGS

As in the case of engravings, so in the case of paintings far greater skill is evinced. Four legs are indicated and an attempt at perspective made. Details such as hair etc. are frequently added (Fig. 23, *3*). It now appears that most of the drawings in "flat-wash" (a sort of silhouette) may be assigned, also, to this time, as well as certain simple bichromes, i.e. figures painted in two colours.

PHASE C

The outline remains wide and deep, but is no longer continuous and considerably more skill is evinced than is the case even in phase B. Some of the drawings show great vigour and beauty (Fig. 24 A.) In this phase, too, considerable attempts were made to give a three-dimensional sense to the art. Actual work in relief was occasionally done and it was to this time that we must assign most of the attempts to touch up natural projections of stalactite (roughly resembling animals in form) by the addition of painted horns or eyes or legs, etc. and so to turn them into actual representations of the animals which the artist desired to figure. A peculiar style in Cantabria includes very fine engravings (little more than scratchings) beautifully made and representing animals' heads (especially hinds) the whole body of the drawing being filled in with fine engraved lines (Fig. 21, *1* and Fig. 24 B).

Three distinct styles of monochrome painting can be recognised, the one a sort of "stump drawing", the second in which the outline consists of a series of carefully made punctuations, the body of the animal itself being sometimes covered with these dots—and the third when the whole body of the animal is well executed in flatwash. In the first of these styles a veritable sense of relief is obtained by what can only be described as shading (Plate VII). The second is somewhat peculiar, and the result is not a little conventionalised. Some examples of this punctuation style may actually date back to the end of phase A, as at La Pasiéga, but the majority would seem to belong rather to phase C (Plate VIII, upper photograph). There are also a number of black outline paintings.

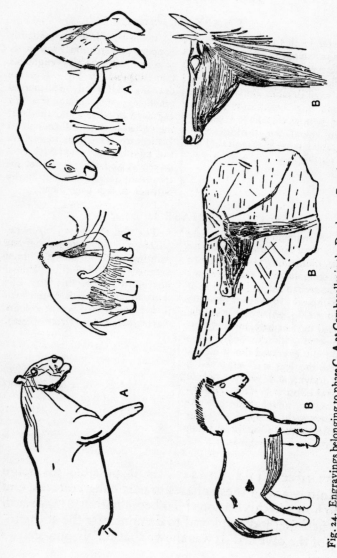

Fig. 24. Engravings belonging to phase C. A at Combarelles in the Dordogne, B at sites in Cantabria; the central figure of a hind engraved on a piece of bone belongs to the home art and dates this special Cantabrian style of phase C.

PHASE C (*continued*)

Later in this phase engravings became smaller and the lines shallower than at its beginning. While the artist frequently shows very considerable skill and the animals are beautifully drawn, there is now somehow a certain lack of vigour, the drawings seeming rather more mechanical (Fig. 21, *1*).

At this time it not infrequently happens that an animal was partly painted and partly engraved. Sometimes, as in Fig. 25, *2* the drawing itself is only in outline, at other times the animal was first engraved in outline and the body then filled in in a uniform colour. Little care was taken to register the painting and engraved lines correctly, and the colour not infrequently fails to come up to the outlines or laps over them.

PHASE D

The engravings are as a rule small, very fine and beautifully made. Something in the nature of suggestion pictures can occasionally be recognised, as in the case of a mammoth from the Font de Gaume (Fig. 26) where it will be noticed the feet are completely unconnected with the body, there being no engraved lines in between, the legs are "suggested", not drawn, and yet the whole general effect is perfect. The engravings are no longer deep as was the case early in phase C (other than the special Cantabrian style) but are mere scratchings.

The fourth phase is *par excellence* the period of polychrome painting and to it have been assigned the beautiful animal figures from Altamira, etc. The skill employed by palaeolithic man in applying the different colours was truly wonderful (frontispiece).

DATING OF THE PHASES. Is it possible to assign definitely any of these phases to particular cultures, and if so how can this be done? To begin with, we may recall the first method employed to demonstrate the authenticity of the cave art. It was shown that at Pair-non-Pair—

Fig. 25. Cave art paintings. 1, Horse in red flat-wash at Altamira, phase C. 2, Bison partly engraved, partly painted in red, at Pindal, and 3, painted bisons at Marsoulas showing various styles, all phase C.

and the same is true at La Grèze, a few miles from Les Eyzies, at Cap Blanc, and at several other sites—the engravings were found sealed in by deposits containing datable stone implements. They must therefore be older than the age of the implements in the deposits that cover them. Straight away then we have an upper date limit and if the engravings in question definitely belong to a style in one of the phases, such an upper limit can be applied to the phase itself. Thus at Pair-non-Pair the engravings belong to a style in phase A and they are covered by upper Aurignacian tools. If they had been drawn by a man in middle Aurignacian times, he would have had to kneel on the floor in order to perform his task; if on the other hand the artist was a "lower Aurignacian", the floor-level at Pair-non-Pair at that time would have been sufficiently low to permit him to work standing up. It is therefore probable that they were the work of lower Aurignacian artists and that phase A should be assigned to this date. Finds at other sites confirm this conclusion.

The second method useful for dating the phases in terms of cultures depends on the finding in the home art of engravings made in the same style as certain of those found on cave walls. Thus at Altamira in lower Magdalenian levels there occur engravings of hinds similar in every way—though of course on a smaller scale—to that peculiar style in phase C mentioned as occurring in Cantabria (Fig. 24, B), and there is every reason to believe that phase C as a whole can be assigned to a lower Magdalenian date. In the same way again the engraving of a horse's hind quarters found in an early Aurignacian level at Hornos de la Peña in Cantabria and identical in many ways with the hind quarters of a small horse engraved on the cave wall near by, the style of which is clearly phase A, demonstrates once again that this phase should be assigned to the Aurignacian period (Figs. 19, 6 and 22, 1).

In this connection one of the most interesting finds that has been made in England concerns a small engraved bone discovered in the Pin Hole Cave at Creswell Crags on the borders of Nottinghamshire and Derbyshire (Plate III). The engraving (Fig. 18, 4) is poorly made and represents in outline a human being. But in many ways it is identical in treatment with a series of engraved human figures that were discovered on the ceiling at Altamira underneath—and therefore older than—the famous polychrome painted frieze. The little human figures at Altamira have long been considered as belonging to phase A and as being Aurignacian in date. Further proof is now added since the engraving at Creswell Crags was found definitely in an Aurignacian milieu.

In the same way, finds at Teyjat in the Dordogne show that to phase C must be assigned a middle Magdalenian date and it is believed that phase D, the heyday of Magdalenian art, must be dated towards the end of Magdalenian times. It will thus be seen that phases A and B are Aurignacian, and phases C and D Magdalenian.

The student must always remember that this grouping into phases is a purely artificial classification. It is not suggested that the scheme given above is entirely comprehensive or final. It differs from that offered in the original edition of this book, but, it is hoped, is nearer the truth in the light of the recent discoveries at Lascaux. (See p. 201.)

All too little attention has, alas, been paid to a study of the cave art from an artist's point of view. The wonderful drawings have been admired by countless visitors and the art itself has been treated by the prehistorian in a purely scientific manner, but the methods employed by the artists and the technique of their craft have not yet been studied on the spot by a modern art critic who could competently give his impressions and discuss the problems in his own art jargon. Such a study would be extremely interesting, both artistically, historically and psychologically, and it is to be hoped that some qualified person will soon undertake it.

A list of the different animals figured is of considerable interest. It includes the bison, ox, reindeer, stag, hind, roebuck, elk, ibex, chamois, wild boar, mammoth, elephant, rhinoceros, horse, lion, fish (including trout, salmon and sea fish), birds (rare, poorly drawn and indeterminate), and man (always poorly drawn). The percentage of these animals occurring in different phases is of some interest, but less important scientifically than might be imagined. It does not by any means follow that the proportion found in the paintings must be the same as that of the animals occurring at the period. In fact in some instances the opposite is the case. As will appear later, it is probable that the drawings were connected with the food supply in the practice of sympathetic magic, and it would almost seem that sometimes the artist portrayed animals that were not the commonest at the time when he was painting. Perhaps he got rather tired of stags' flesh and hoped that the supply of reindeer meat might be increased! But once again such specialised studies need much more research work; their possibilities are only mentioned here to stimulate the student to undertake such investigations.

VISITING THE CAVES. As it may chance that some readers of this book may have an opportunity of visiting

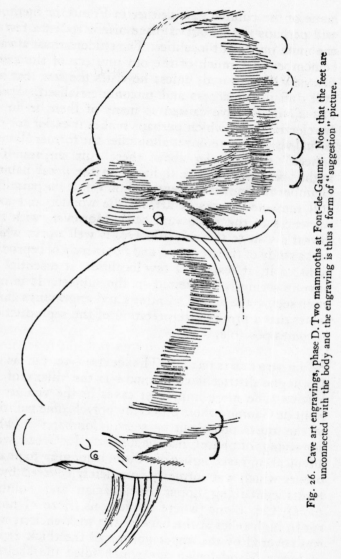

Fig. 26. Cave art engravings, phase D. Two mammoths at Font-de-Gaume. Note that the feet are unconnected with the body and the engraving is thus a form of "suggestion" picture.

some of the painted caves either in France or Spain, it
will perhaps not be out of place briefly to list a few of
the more important localities. The student must always
remember that much of the old mystery of the caves
has now disappeared, unless he visits the few that are
still difficult of access and uncommercialised. *Syndi-
cats d'initiatif* have caused so many of them to be lit
by electric light, which perhaps makes it easier for the
casual visitor but removes altogether the former "atmosphere" which hung about these cult shrines. The
author remembers once lighting up the great painted
chamber at Niaux with Verey lights. While the paintings
still remained works of art, all the wonder and awe-
someness of the place vanished! However, with this
caveat a visit to the painted caves is well worth while;
and a study of the art *in situ*, and not merely of reproductions of it, at least at a few localities, is essential for
anyone seriously interested in the subject. It is only
after seeing the actual paintings and engravings themselves that a proper interpretation of the reproductions
becomes possible.

DORDOGNE DISTRICT. The centre—so far as the
Dordogne district is concerned—is the village of Les
Eyzies. The more important caves in the vicinity are
Font de Gaume (where especially polychrome paintings
of the fourth phase can be seen); Combarelles (where
engravings of phase C may be studied); La Grèze (where
a typical engraved figure of a bison belonging to phase A
occurs which was formerly completely covered by deposits containing upper Aurignacian and Solutrean
tools); Cap Blanc (where the famous frieze of horses,
cut in high relief at the back of the rock-shelter, which
was covered by the upper portion of the thick deposits
of lower Magdalenian age which filled the shelter, is
visible, the frieze had included a bison but this became

detached from the wall and has been removed); Gorge d'Enfer (where a salmon has been cut in relief on the roof of a small home site); La Mouthe (of little interest except from a historical point of view—see paragraph on authenticity). The cave of Cabrerets, not so far from Cahors in the Corrèze, is also well worth a visit, and so, too, very specially, is the recently found cave at Lascaux near Montignac some 30 km. upstream from Les Eyzies. This marvellous discovery was made by chance during the war by some boys whose dog disappeared, while hunting, into what turned out to be not a rabbit hole but an immense cave that has shown us a magnificent series of Aurignacian paintings and some engravings. Here for the first time it has been possible to study scores of beautiful pictures, some in outline, others in flat-wash and others again in bichrome which all belong to the very dawn of art. The new discoveries corrected in places previous assumptions and it is now realised how much more elaborate was the art of the Aurignacians than had been thought and how many more styles there were; and the fourfold scheme of phases (pp. 189–97) owes some of its current rearrangement to Lascaux. In this cave there are various kinds of animals depicted, oxen, stags, horses, etc., and also signs which are sometimes quite elaborate. The feeling of vigour and movement given by the pictures is most arresting. The oxen seem to be pounding along, the ponies are certainly trotting and some of the stags may even be swimming. At the end of the cave there is a natural pit some 20 ft. deep giving access to a lower gallery where paintings also occur. Here there is a disembowelled bison, a contented-looking rhinoceros, a conventionalised man, and a bird sign on the end of a staff. Naturally we can only guess at what it was all intended to represent. Occasionally animals are depicted with their tongues out which recall the scene at

Alpera in the eastern Spanish rock-shelter art-groups where a stag with its tongue out faces an archer (Fig. 29).

Lascaux can indeed be described as an Aurignacian Altamira. There the Magdalenian animals are perhaps better painted and each shows better its own special character. But they are all static. The Aurignacian animals at Lascaux are alive and dynamic.

PYRENEES DISTRICT. From Tarascon-en-Ariège the great caverns of Niaux and Bédheilhac can be visited, and, further afield, and with the permission and collaboration of their respective owners so, too, can the important caves of Portel, Tuc d'Audubert and Trois Frères. Marsoulas and Gargas are easily reached from Salies de Sarlat (Haute Garonne) and Montréjeau respectively. It is in the latter that the student can study the mutilated hands, and also some very interesting and complex panels of engravings belonging to phases A and B (Fig. 22, 2).

CANTABRIA. The best centre for visting these sites is Puente Viesgo (Plate II), a village on the railway from Santander to Ontañeda. The important painted caves, Castillo and Pasiéga, and the newly-found Las Monedas are all close to Puente Viesgo itself. Altamira itself, close to Santillana del Mar, is but a short car-drive away through Torrelavega, and Hornos de la Peña is also not far distant. In the latter case a short walk is necessary to reach the cave which is some little distance from the nearest motor road at Tarriba. While Altamira is of course the classic site at which to study the polychrome paintings of Magdalenian times, the careful searcher who has already visited Lascaux will also be able to locate and recognise the head of an ox of the earlier style and much fainter than the polychromes which in part cross above it. It is a very lovely drawing. Hornos de la Peña can show us some very fine engravings belonging to phase B.

Chapter XII

MOTIVES UNDERLYING THE PRODUCTION
OF THE ART

CONSIDERABLE controversy has raged as to
the motives underlying the production of the
wonderful palaeolithic art which we have just
been describing. There have been some authorities who
have urged strongly that it was merely a manifestation
of the artistic temperament among a naturally artistic
people; that artists have an inner compulsion to express
themselves in some way or other and that in this
particular instance it took the form of pictorial representations of the animals that roamed about the world
in front of their homes. Others again have argued that
the love of beautiful surroundings inherent in an artistic
people required that many of their tools should be
decorated and their cave walls beautified. Others have
suggested (and this of course only applies really to the
cave art) that the drawings were made to commemorate
successes in hunting. Others again have seen behind
the art a utilitarian purpose involving a form of sympathetic magic to ensure the continuance of a constant
food supply.

Briefly, it would seem permissible to classify all the
possible motive theories under three headings: decoration, self-expression, sympathetic magic. We will
examine the cave art from these points of view.

It will generally be found that the protagonists
arguing for one motive or another have solely taken
into account the drawings themselves, but this surely

omits half the evidence. Not only should the art itself be considered but also the circumstances under which it occurs. Before discussing which of these motives is likely to be the true one, then, it will be well to re-visit the caves, taking special account of any relevant information to be derived from a study of the occurrence and positions of the drawings.

SUPERPOSITIONS. We have already noted the essential difference between a phase and a style, and the occurrence of superpositions of phases is not necessarily surprising. Different phases belong to very different periods, and as the amount of wall space really suitable for painting or engraving in even a large cave is frequently surprisingly restricted, one need not wonder that the artists of one phase seem to have often completely disregarded the efforts of their predecessors, and it does not necessarily follow from this that motives of decoration or self-expression must be ruled out. Where, however, we have superpositions of figures in the same style, as for example at Teyjat in the Dordogne, the engravings of animals being made one on top of another with no reference to each other, and yet all of them being more or less contemporary (Fig. 21), it is hard to see anything in the nature of an attempt at decoration. Incidentally at this particular site it is not the walls of the cave that are engraved but just a chance block of stalactite that had fallen from the roof. The frequence of superpositions, however, while inimical to the decoration motive theory, is less so to that of expression. If a prehistoric artist on a bright spring morning felt an inward urge to draw a cave bear, it does not necessarily follow that he would hold his hand because somebody a short time previously had covered the best "canvas" with the figure of a reindeer. Personally, I think our chance artist would choose another canvas, but it is possible to take up the attitude that he would care little whether anybody had been there before him or not.

POSITION. Having noted the occurrence of superpositions of more or less contemporary figures, we may next take account of the positions in the caves of a number of the drawings. In the first place, attention may be drawn to such a cave as Niaux, near Tarascon-en-Ariège, south of Toulouse, where no painting is found on the walls (although many of them are suitable for the purpose) until almost 800 yards of often difficult going straight into the heart of the hill have been accomplished. Naturally such a site demands elaborately organised artificial illumination; to-day this great cave is not one to be visited with a bit of candle, or even with a bicycle lamp. It is difficult to imagine our chance spring-drunk artist, impelled to express himself in pictorial representation, seizing a brand from the fire and scrambling to the far end of this immense mysterious cavern in order to paint one of the bison, ibex, or horses that are found there.

Again, at the celebrated cave of Font-de-Gaume, close to Les Eyzies, there is a narrow crevice at the end of the main gallery, so narrow that in recent times it has been blocked up by a gateway to avoid the damage to the paintings on its walls which would inevitably have happened had tourists been allowed freely to push their way along it. On penetrating some distance into this crevice and looking upwards, a very fine engraving of a lion and a still finer painting of a woolly rhinoceros (Fig. 23, 3) can be seen many feet above the surface of the ground on the left-hand wall. To get to these figures it is necessary to use a step ladder, or to scramble up on the shoulders of a companion. The crevice is so narrow that in no case can one get more than a few feet away from the drawings, and photographs of them can only be obtained with the aid of mirrors. Nor can it be argued that the floor-level in the cave has been lowered by denudation at a date subsequent to the making of the drawings, for palaeolithic paintings are equally found on the walls of the crevice close to the present floor-level. That anybody impelled by the wish to draw the figure of an animal should penetrate to the end of Font-de-Gaume, where of course artificial lights are essential, continue to the end of the crevice and clamber up so as to make these pictures in this awkward situation, where they never could be properly seen, is surely unthinkable.

It has already been stated in Chapter 1 that palaeolithic man never inhabited the depths of caves, and this for obvious reasons. In certain circumstances it is true his industries are found in the mouths of caves and it sometimes happens, as at Castillo, that the walls of the galleries behind have been covered with paintings and engravings; but in a great many examples this is not the case and the painted and engraved caves are completely unconnected with any home sites. No cinders have been found in them and the chance implement that has been collected was almost certainly just part of the artist's bag of tools. If the caves, then, were never used as homes it is a little difficult to say why their walls should have been emblazoned for the purposes of decoration. The argument from position is thus inimical both to the decoration and expression motive theories.

SIGNS AND HANDS (Fig. 27). In studying the cave art we are continually coming across examples of painted signs (tectiforms, scutiforms, etc.), and these surely can hardly be said to be decorative! Further, such signs are often especially concealed in the most obscure portions of the cave; at Castillo, for example, there is a small alcove which can be easily missed by even a careful explorer, on the sloping ceiling of which occur tectiforms that one can only see by lying on one's back and wriggling into it. Or again, in the neighbouring cave of La Pasiéga there is a long gallery full of excellent figures of animals. At its end this gallery turns sharply to the left and becomes merely a narrow crack hardly to be entered sideways; but the walls of this crack are covered with tectiform signs. Again, at the cave of Bolao not far from Llanes, in northern Spain, there is no art except for a group of red painted tectiforms on the low arched ceiling near a particularly good spring of water within the cave. These tectiforms are thought by some investigators to represent constructions—either real "houses" or "soul-houses" for the dead. Others have thought them to be traps in the form of pits in the ground, lightly covered and concealed by boughs, into which the desired animals might fall or be driven. At Bolao, as we have seen, they were perhaps connected with the available supply of good water.

The occurrence of painted hands of both the positive and negative variety must also be remembered; more especially the mutilated hands at Gargas where, in a great many instances, one or more joints of one or more of the fingers are missing (Fig. 27, c). The human hand to-day plays a considerable part in the ritual usages, not only of modern primitive peoples but also of ourselves. We bless and salute by raising the hand in various ways;

equally in cursing we point the hand at the enemy; while the Moslem often wears a small image of a hand round his neck to avert the evil eye. Such examples can be multiplied. There is even modern analogy for the mutilation by the removal of joints of the fingers, this being done to divert a present evil and to satisfy the malignant powers which are causing it. It is, of course, dangerous to take any modern explanation and apply it to prehistoric times. Besides, as has been said, there is more than one ritual use of the human hand current in our own day, but at least it would seem difficult to argue that these paintings, sometimes anatomically mutilated, can have anything to do with either a desire for decoration, or for self-expression.

ARROWS. It sometimes happens that arrows have been drawn on the animal-figures in the painted caves. It might be argued, of course, that here at least we have the representation of some hunting scene and that the artist has desired to commemorate his prowess in the chase. But there is at least one figure in the cave at Niaux which, while it does not completely rule out this explanation, yet makes it less satisfactory. Just beyond the great cross-roads in the heart of the mountain, on the right-hand side of the passage and on the floor, which here consists of sand slightly hardened by stalagmite, under an overhanging wall, can be seen the engraving of a bison. In the middle of the bison's body are three small holes close together, quite clearly natural in origin, and resulting from the dropping of water from the overhanging wall at some time or other. These little holes must have been noted by the artist, for he has as it were indicated each of them with a little engraved arrow, and then drawn his bison around

Fig. 27. Cave art. A, Various kinds of tectiforms. B, Engravings, "maca-roni", phase A. C, Negative mutilated hands at Gargas. D, Club-like signs. E, "inscription" at La Pasiéga.

them (Fig. 28). If the artist had merely been desiring to commemorate a successful hunt, he would surely not have taken the trouble to make this exquisite little engraving on the floor in an obscure part of the cave; he would have made a large painting on a more accessible panel which he and his friends could come and admire with greater ease.

ABSENCE OF SCENES. The absence of scenes is very striking and almost complete in the palaeolithic art; and almost invariably when they do occur they are confined to two figures only, and the number of even these can really be counted on the fingers of two hands. The best known example perhaps is that of the two reindeer, male and female, at Font-de-Gaume, where the female is kneeling with her head down and the male animal is shown bending forward, apparently preparatory to licking her face. It is a charming picture of animal life. The comparative absence of human figures is also remarkable and when they do occur they are always extremely badly drawn. Surely if there had been any desire to commemorate a successful hunt, we might have expected to find definite scenes representing the chase; for example, a vast mammoth or reindeer surrounded by hunters giving it death blows!

Finally attention must be drawn to the two *mises-en-scène* at the Tuc d'Audoubert and the Trois Frères. An attempt must, therefore, be made briefly to describe these important sites. The original ancient entrance to the Tuc d'Audoubert has probably been masked by a subsequent landslide and the explorer to-day enters, as it were, by a back door. To begin with, one has to row up a little stream that issues from a cavern. After penetrating into the hill for a short distance, one lands

Fig. 28. Cave art. The "sorcerer" at the Trois Frères cave; and the wounded bison at Niaux.

and finds oneself in a beautiful vestibule hung with milk-white stalactites. Here some excellent engravings belonging to phase C (lower Magdalenian) can be seen in a corner of the chamber. On mounting a ladder to the roof and climbing up a sort of natural chimney, a passage is reached, very up and down and often very narrow. Indeed, the first explorers found this passage completely blocked by stalactite which had to be destroyed before further penetration was possible. After a time the passage opens out into a gallery which is rather damp, there being a good deal of clay on the floor. At one place the impress of a naked human foot is visible and a number of cave-bear teeth carefully collected and placed on a little projection of the wall can be seen. At the end of the gallery, probably not so very far from where the original entrance of the cave must have been, leaning against a natural block of rock are two bisons modelled in clay. In front is the female, behind is the male (Plate V). Both are about two feet long. Near by on the right there is a semicircular depression forming a sort of small amphitheatre, and on the clay surface of this depression can be seen marks as if somebody had been dancing on his heels round a tiny hillock that is to be seen in the centre. Near by on the floor is also a very nice engraving of a harpoon. The whole gives one a strong impression that the site had been used for some cult or ritual purpose, and further that the locality was not merely used once by chance but was a definite cave cult-shrine.

The cave of the Trois Frères opens not far from the entrance to the Tuc d'Audoubert. But the easiest method of penetration is through a small passage about the size of a large rabbit-hole which leads out from the end of a small cave called Enlène, where a very fine

PLATE VII

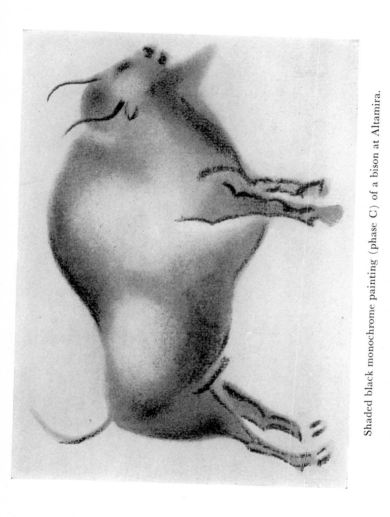

Shaded black monochrome painting (phase C) of a bison at Altamira.

Magdalenian site has been excavated, containing some excellent pieces of home art. After penetrating the hill for some distance the passage bifurcates once or twice. We follow the left-hand road, and, after passing by the little alcove on the right-hand side, where occurs the engraving of a lion and the graver that made it, which has already been mentioned, we shall find ourselves descending into a small chamber, the walls of which, as high as a man can comfortably reach, are covered with innumerable engravings of many different kinds of animals. At the end of this chamber there is a sort of natural tunnel, itself engraved, after following which for a short distance a passage appears to the right, and this, mounting rapidly, turns back on itself and opens out as a sort of window about 12 feet or more above the ground-level of the engraved chamber just described. Anyone standing in this window or natural pulpit dominates the chamber, and of course any audience within it. On the rock wall just beside the pulpit there is a figure of the sorcerer himself, masked, with the head of a stag and a long tail, but clearly human, as is seen by looking at his legs and feet (Fig. 28). The figure is partly engraved, partly painted. The position of the pictured sorcerer dominating the little decorated chamber and the audience within it, close alongside the natural pulpit where the real live sorcerer would stand, makes it impossible to believe that the whole thing is not connected with some ritual; and clearly, all the art manifestations that occur here are part and parcel of whatever cult ceremony or ritual it was, which must have taken place.

These two sites are especially significant for our purpose; not only must we agree that everything hangs together, that each individual engraving is part of an intentional whole, but further, the fact of the "pulpit" at the Trois Frères, where the real artist-medicine-man-priest could stand side by side with the painted sorcerer, argues strongly for the suggestion that the various figures were not drawn by chance artists, but that the whole is the product of professionals and was drawn by them for some ritual purpose. Further argument in favour of this theory that the art was the work of professionals is furnished by the fact that the changes in phase occur throughout wide areas at the same time; and it would seem to follow from this that there must have been definite schools where the technique of drawing and painting was learned, and that these schools were closely connected with one another, with the result that even allowing for local variation there is a very considerable similarity in the cave art wherever it is found.

When all these considerations are taken into account it will probably be seen that neither the decoration nor the expression theories are really tenable. What can we say as to the explanation of sympathetic magic? Merely to say that sympathetic magic is the motive underlying the production of the cave art is obviously insufficient, and it becomes necessary to define more closely exactly what we mean. But it is just here that the problem becomes somewhat complicated, and the student will find that in order to understand the matter clearly he has to consider the question from various aspects. In the first place obviously prehistoric man's life must have been considerably simpler than is our own to-day, and problems of the necessities of life must have loomed very large in his thoughts. Such things as birth and death were doubtless always fearful mysteries, but above all, as in the hunting stage of civilisation serious storage of food is impossible, the problem of the food supply must have been an ever-present anxiety. We have already noted the occurrence of statuettes of apparently pregnant women, and we have seen in a previous chapter that there is evidence for the existence of palaeolithic ceremonial burial. It is now suggested that the cave art was closely connected with the problem of the food supply.

Human beings react to perceptions: bury your face in a bed of stinging nettles and you will instantly remove it. In such a case there is little or no delay between perception and reaction. If this were always so, if no delay occurred between the two, humanity would be purely automatic; for it is just during the delay between perception and reaction that our emotional existence comes into play. Such delay may be involuntary or voluntary. To give a homely example, we may be hungry but there may be no food in the house, or again, we may be hungry and there may be plenty of food but the guests whom we have invited have not yet arrived. In either case, however, it is the period of delay between perception and reaction which gives rise to an increase of emotional tension. By sitting on a safety valve, an increased internal pressure is produced. Now with many modern primitive peoples it is known that such an increase in emotional pressure gives rise to mimetic representations of what is desired. Instances of this can be multiplied; there are people whose well-being depends on the seasonal rainfall, and if this is delayed they will play-act rain-making with the help of a watering can. There are others, who live by hunting, who are dependent on the seasonal return of the game and these will act a hunting scene. As a rule such mimetic representations are bound up with dancing, the whole forming an elaborate ceremonial. Indeed, for many human beings dancing is still the recognised way of getting rid of superfluous emotion. Just after the 1914–18 war, after four years of tension, Great Britain went dancing mad! It is probable that prehistoric man also indulged in ceremonial dances when game was scarce and the struggle for existence became acute.

But in upper palaeolithic times among certain peoples in the extreme west of Europe it would seem that the ritual in all probability was bound up with the pictorial representations of animals. Primitive peoples frequently fail to distinguish clearly between the object and an image made of it, and if, after some dancing ceremonial, the artist-medicine-man-priest could conduct the hunter (or hunters) to the heart of the cave and show him portrayed upon the walls the spirits of the desired animal duly captured by him with his arrows in its side, then confidence in the success of the ritual, and therefore in the next hunt, would be engendered—and in hunting confidence is half the battle. It seems to me that once again the situation in which the art occurs must be remembered. Many of the painted caves are really very terrifying places; the silence is intense, broken only occasionally by a distant boom when a drop of water falls from the roof into some silent pool below. The darkness is complete, while a feeble illumination only serves to intensify the mysteriousness of half-concealed passages and alcoves that branch off to right and left; everything is unfamiliar and weird. What must have been the effect of all this on the emotions of a group of Magdalenians led on ever deeper into the hill by the sorcerer—a man who by temperament, training and custom is no longer troubled by the strange surroundings? Surely by the time our party had reached the paintings they would be in a suggestible state of mind which could be readily influenced by the officiating sorcerer? Surely he would be able to inspire them with confidence as he shows them the animals that they need for food whose spirits he has already captured and whose bodies he affirms they will be slaughtering in the near future? Couéism if you like, but M. Coué invented nothing new; throughout all ages the medicine-man, or sorcerer, or priest has existed. From one point of view it may be said that he battens on the superstitions and weaknesses of his people, but on the other hand he is often the leader who frequently inspires them with confidence and courage, and without whom the emotional life of the social group lacks all direction.

It would seem, then, that in sympathetic magic as so outlined we have a reasonable explanation of the problem of the cave art which explains not only the presence of the drawings themselves but also the reason why they occur in such apparently extraordinary situations. Also we can understand why it is that the art is not the product of the chance hunter but the result of professional effort, probably trained in schools, where instruction in drawing the various animals would have been given. Of course again and again effective ritual degenerates gradually into the performance of merely meaningless rites; and whereas at first the mysterious penetration into the depths of the caves must have been a necessary part of the suggesting process, in time this might come to be omitted and the rite practised simply for its own sake, probably in some more convenient situation. By custom the connection with the caves would still be maintained but a more accessible *venue*, perhaps nearer the entrance, would be selected. Actually the circumstances at the Tuc d'Audoubert would seem to admit of some such explanation.

HOME ART. While it would seem fairly certain, then, that such utilitarian motives underlay the production of the cave art, it should never be forgotten that if upper palaeolithic man in western Europe had not belonged to an artistic race, the particular kind of sympathetic magic practised by him would have taken a different form. While, however, we cannot, as has been seen, admit either decoration or desire for self-expression as motives for the art in the cave-temples or, as we have perhaps more correctly called them, cult-shrines, the problem is very different when we come to the home sites. Let us firstly consider the art found at such places as Cap Blanc, Gorge d'Enfer or Le Roc.

In the first of these it will be remembered that the back wall of the inhabited rock-shelter was sculptured into a frieze of horses and a bison, whose date is usually assigned to the lower Magdalenian period, though it may be somewhat earlier. At the second we find a sculptured salmon on the roof of the little rock-shelter which had also been inhabited. At the third locality there is a frieze of sculptured animals of Solutrean date forming a sort of revetment around a semicircular area cut into the sloping hillside, in this case not actually at the home site but very close by. There is no reason to deny—certainly in the case of the first two—that this art may have been purely decorative. The owner of the rock-shelter in each case may have wished to make his domain more beautiful; he has certainly shòwn very considerable skill. Perhaps he was himself the local artist-medicine-man-priest: that of course we shall never know. Even at Le Roc, although the site is slightly apart from the actual living home, there is no reason to deny a decoration motive, though in this case modern investigators in describing the site have ventured to use the word "sanctuary". The point is that when we get away from the cave cult-shrines we cannot affirm that any form of magic is necessarily involved, and this is especially so in the case of the home art; for it would seem more than likely that a great deal of what we find must have been simply made for pleasure. Of course in some instances the drawings on weapons may have been made to render these tools more effective. Furthermore, female statuettes—the "Venuses" of Aurignacian date—would certainly seem to be connected with some fertility cult, though it is perfectly possible that palaeolithic man also regarded them as works of art. On the other hand a great many of the little decorated objects, little engraved plaques of stone, etc., with a hole for suspension purposes, were probably nothing more or less than ornaments; perhaps presents from a man to his wife. So in the case of the home art, while not denying that some of it may have been made for magic purposes, there is no reason to doubt that much of it must have been simply due to a desire for decoration or self-expression.

Two further ideas suggest themselves. It would seem unlikely that even the artist-medicine-man-priest should have been able so incredibly skilfully to paint the animals in the caves from memory only. Even if he had instruction as to the technique of his craft, the results are so surprisingly life-like—take for example the ceiling at Altamira where each bison has a character of its own, no two being alike in this respect—that it would seem reasonable to suggest the possibility that he first made sketches from nature and that these were afterwards used in the production of the cave drawings. The modern artist starting to-day on a big canvas will often make such a small sketch first. Some of the drawings found in the homes may be these sketches. As we have already noted, at Hornos de la Peña in north Spain, the engraving of a horse can be seen near the entrance; within a few yards of it in an Aurignacian deposit there was discovered an engraving on bone of the hind quarters of a horse amazingly similar in its lines to that engraved on the cave wall close by (Figs. 19, 6 and 22, *1*).

Finally, as we have spoken much about schools for the artist, we must not omit to remember that at such places we might expect to find the practice "slates" of the budding draughtsmen. These would be likely to take the form of pieces of bone or stone covered with attempts at engravings. It is significant that, while at a site like La Madeleine only finished products occur, at Les Eyzies there are any number of such crude attempts. Are we to consider that at the rock-shelter of Les Eyzies there used to be so many thousands of years ago a prototype of our schools of art of to-day?

ADDENDUM. Another interesting locality is the cave of Candamo some miles from Oviedo in North Spain. Here there is a large chamber in which is a considerable area of painted wall. High up near the roof is a small alcove, itself full of paintings, which can only be reached after a considerable scramble. Anyone in this little alcove would dominate a congregation below in front of the large painted panel of the great chamber. In some respects the situation recalls that at the Trois Frères.

Chapter XIII

ROCK-SHELTER ART IN EASTERN SPAIN

A VERY important series of rock-shelter paintings
has been discovered in eastern Spain which,
while in many ways quite unlike the art we have
already described, is nevertheless very interesting. The
sites where the paintings—engravings are more than
rare—are found, fringe the eastern coast of the peninsula, never occurring more than 75 miles or so from
the sea. While a correlation in time with the upper
palaeolithic cave art of south France and north Spain
can be made, no cultural connections with the north
can be discovered and it is to Africa that we have to
look for the origin of this art group.

The rock-shelters are never of any great depth, so
the paintings can be seen by the light of day. At first
sight it would seem somewhat astonishing that paintings
in the open air, only slightly protected by a rock-
shelter, should have survived since palaeolithic times,
but in this connection one or two things must be
remembered. In the first place eastern and south-
eastern Spain are very dry areas, and probably have
been so for a very long time. Furthermore, the paintings
which have survived form probably only a small proportion of the number which formerly existed, and they
certainly have only been preserved because the particular rock-shelters have protected them from undue
weathering. That such protection has been given can
indeed be demonstrated. The rock-shelters occur in

limestone, a material composed of calcium carbonate but invariably containing a certain amount of iron as an impurity. If the surface of the limestone is exposed for any length of time to the atmosphere, the iron salts become oxidised and the limestone becomes pinkish-brown in colour. When moisture is present, however, and there is considerable condensation and subsequent evaporation of water vapour due to daily changes of temperature, the growth of a grey lichen is promoted. Indeed the grey colour of most limestone hills is not so much due to the colour of the rock as to this lichen.

Now should much condensation and evaporation of water vapour have taken place in a painted rock-shelter not only would the walls have been eroded and the paintings thus destroyed, but, further, the growth of lichen would have been engendered, and this, besides hiding the paintings, would have tended to destroy them too, the small rootlets of the plant disintegrating the surface of the rock. Should, however, the rock-shelter have remained dry, owing to its general position and situation, then no lichen would have been able to grow and no eroding of the surface of the rock-wall would have taken place. Moreover, in this case, there being no protective covering of lichen, oxidation of the iron salts would take place, with the result that the wall of the rock-shelter would appear pinkish-brown in colour. It is invariably true that only where this colouration is apparent do paintings occur, and therefore it can be confidently affirmed that weathering has not been able to operate at the sites where the art has been preserved. Frequently, too, something of the nature of a very thin film of stalactite has formed over the paintings, doubtless owing to the oozing out of moisture from within the

Fig. 29. Rock-shelter art in eastern Spain. Hunting scene at Alpéra
and stag at Cretas.

limestone (cf. p. 181), and this itself has further protected the paintings. Often a careful damping of the rock-shelter wall with a sponge will make the paintings appear much clearer; this is because the refractive index of water being near to that of stalactite the latter, when wetted, becomes somewhat more translucent in the same way as does a piece of ground glass when placed in a bowl of water.

The following differences between this eastern Spanish art group and that which we have been considering hitherto can be noted. In the first place, while it is not untrue to say that the eastern Spanish artists were naturalistic in their treatment of subjects, their drawings are very different from those of the northern group. The technique recalls much more that of a Japanese picture, as will be readily seen on reference to Figs. 29 and 30. Yet it should be noted that such anatomical details as the stag's cloven hoof and so on are always carefully indicated.

Next we may note that human beings are frequently depicted. Whereas hitherto figures representing the human form have been exceedingly rare and invariably poorly drawn, now they are found in profusion, and although the treatment is very schematic, much more so than in the case of the animals depicted, they are by no means wooden in appearance, but represent live and active individuals. We may notice, too, that some of the women are evidently wearing clothes, while the men sometimes have headdresses. Bows and arrows are frequently in their hands, and this fact alone differentiates the two art groups. While there is nothing to suggest that the upper palaeolithic folk of France and north Spain had not discovered the possibilities of the bow and arrow—indeed, certain bone points found at

Castillo possibly were used as arrow tips—there is no proof that this weapon had been developed by them, at any rate it is never figured in their drawings. In eastern Spain, however, it is often shown.

In the third place we can note the frequent occurrence of scenes. The most famous of these is of course that found at Cogul, where a number of clothed women are seen surrounding a small naked male figure (Fig. 30). People who wish to interpret everything prehistoric in terms of some phallic cult have always seized upon this scene as proving their point. One or two considerations, however, should be kept in mind. The male figure is very small, much smaller than that of the women surrounding him, so that he represents a boy rather than a man; also the penis is not in an erect attitude. It would seem more likely that some initiation rite is being depicted rather than that a representation of a phallic scene was intended. Usually, however, it is hunting scenes that are portrayed. A charming little example occurs at Alpéra where a hunter is shown with bow in hand and arrow strung, facing a stag who seems to be quite indifferent to the danger, since he has actually put his tongue out at the hunter (Fig. 29). A charmingly humorous touch this, which seems to bring us very close to these ancient artists and to bridge the gap of thousands of years. Above is seen another group, also showing a hunter and stag, but this time the arrow has flown and the wounded stag with his back to the hunter seems to be walking sorrowfully away. Actually it is not the same stag that is represented in each case, as can be seen by observing their antlers; we are, therefore, dealing with a composite group and not as it were successive cinematograph pictures of the same event. At a site in the Barranco de

Valtorta in the province of Castillon there can be seen paintings depicting a veritable battue. A line of archers is shown, towards whom a number of animals are clearly being driven. As has been said before, in the cave art of the northern group, scenes are more than rare and when they do occur two figures at most are concerned.

Finally, in eastern Spain the drawings themselves are as a rule altogether smaller than those we have previously had to deal with; not that small figures do not frequently occur in the northern group, but taken as a whole the eastern Spanish art is drawn on an altogether smaller scale.

The dating of this art group depends on three considerations. In the first place there frequently occur, on the walls of the same rock-shelters where there are examples of eastern Spanish art, highly conventionalised and symbolic figures—especially in the south-east of the Peninsula. These figures are fresher in appearance and belong to another art group altogether (Spanish Art Group III). They can be fairly accurately dated to the Copper Age of that region. It occasionally happens that superpositions of paintings of the eastern Spanish art (Spanish Art Group II) with some of these of the Copper Age are found, in which case it invariably happens that figures belonging to the latter are painted over those of the former group. This at least gives us an upper limit for dating purposes.

Secondly, among the animals depicted are a number of species that no longer survive in this region. Thus in a rock-shelter facing the little village of Cogul, which is situated on the Rio Set about 11 miles to the south of Lérida in north-east Spain, there occurs the figure of a bison. Although the painting

Fig. 30. Rock-shelter art in eastern Spain. Ritual scene at Cogul. A, Elk at the Cueva del Queso, Alpéra. B, Rhinoceros at Minateda.

is very faded, some years ago when the present writer visited Cogul he satisfied himself that it really was a bison that the artist had intended to depict. It need not be stressed that bison do not roam about in Spain to-day and have not done so since pleistocene times. Again at Minateda—a rock-shelter not far from a halt on the railway line between Chinchilla and Hellín—it has been claimed that a reindeer occurs. While some people might doubt this interpretation, there is no question as to the occurrence at the same site of a figure of a rhinoceros (Fig. 30 B). A single horn on its nose is very clearly marked, and, although the animal is drawn on a very small scale, there can be no doubt as to what was intended. Again, at the rock-shelter of Tortosilla, which can be seen above the cortijo (a Spanish farmhouse) some distance along the same ridge, at the end of which opens the famous rock-shelter of Alpéra,[1] there is a scene depicting a hunter armed with an arrow facing an animal with horns and ears. The horns rise straight up and bend rather forwards, while the ears are directed backwards. There is only one animal with such characteristics and that is the chamois, and the reader does not need reminding that chamois do not to-day roam about the province of Albacete in south Spain. Close to the rock-shelter of Alpéra itself is another site known as the Cueva del Queso (= grotto of the cheese). Here can be seen among a number of paintings the head of what was undoubtedly intended to be an elk with typical nose and palmate antler (Fig. 30 A). Once again we have an animal depicted which no longer exists in the district and has not done so for a very long time. This evidence alone

[1] Both sites are only a few miles from the village and railway station of Alpéra.

PLATE VIII

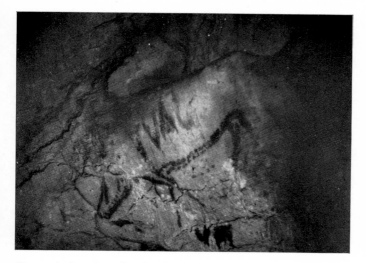

Cave painting of a red ox in the cave of Covalanas above Ramalès in Cantabria.

Two black bisons at Niaux.

suggests that the eastern Spanish art, in part at any rate, must be assigned to late pleistocene times.[1]

Finally, examples of paintings drawn in the eastern Spanish style have been found in certain French and north Spanish caves associated with the northern art. For example, at Portel, a cave in the Pyrenees, there occurs a small painted horse which recalls certain figures representing the same animal at a site (Cantos de la Visera) near Yecla in the province of Murcia, which the present writer had the luck to discover many years ago. Again, the treatment of the antlers of certain figures of stags, which can be seen both at Portel and at La Pasiéga in Cantabria, also resembles that employed by the eastern Spanish artists. Lastly in the home art at a site near Sergeac, in the Dordogne, there has been unearthed a block of limestone on which is painted a stag (Fig. 19,7), many features of which somewhat recall those seen in the eastern Spanish art group. See, too, Lascaux, p. 202.

While therefore it is apparent that a pleistocene age must be postulated for some at any rate of the eastern Spanish paintings, they are not all of one date. Unfortunately, little can be said on this matter at present as a good deal of further work is required. At Minateda no less than 13 different layers of paintings can be distinguished by studying the superpositions that there occur. The site indeed yields us a veritable palimpsest. However, the results of Professor Breuil's work at this site cannot yet be applied at other places, and to make any subdivisions in the eastern Spanish group is at present premature. It would seem obvious, however, from even a cursory study of the paintings in a number

[1] It has been suggested that a particular figure at Alpéra might possibly be that of a dog. I must say this seemed to me very doubtful and certainly it might just as well be that of a wolf.

of sites that several totally different styles occur and
doubtless these correspond to different periods of
time.

Two problems remain to be considered. Firstly, the
origin of this art group and the people responsible for
it; and secondly, the motives underlying its production.
Excavations undertaken in the painted rock-shelters
have yielded little; no hearths have been found and
tools are more than rare. Any implements that have
been discovered suggest rather Capsian than upper
palaeolithic affinities, but, unfortunately, the evidence
is by no means precise. The style of the art itself, however, matches closely that found on the walls of certain
rock-shelters in parts of Africa; indeed an almost exact
counterpart of the eastern Spanish art group is found
as far south as Southern Rhodesia. It is, of course,
a long trek from Southern Rhodesia to eastern Spain,
but one or two intervening links have been discovered.
The most important of these occurs in the rock-shelter
of In-Ezzan[1] in central Sahara, a little to the north
of the Tropic of Cancer. The site lies some 1800 miles
east of the Nile and 1000 miles south-east of the Straits
of Gibraltar. The paintings found there are not all of
one age, but the earlier group closely recalls in style
the art found in eastern Spain and Southern Rhodesia.
It would seem possible, then, to suggest that in late
pleistocene times, from a cultural point of view, the
Spanish peninsula south of the Pyrenees and the Cordillera Cantabrica was really a part of Africa; that the
cultures were Capsian rather than upper palaeolithic,
and that Capsian man was responsible for the art. That
influences from the north filtered south along the
eastern Spanish coast-line has recently been proved by

[1] See *L'Anthropologie*, tome XXXVI, Nos. 5–6, 1926.

Dr Pericot of Valencia, who has been excavating a cave in those regions and has found a Solutrean[1] level on which rests a bed containing an undoubted Magdalenian industry, including examples of home art of the northern kind. But there is as yet no reason to consider that any very great penetration of upper palaeolithic cultures southwards into the Spanish peninsula ever took place. Dr Pericot's find, however, is very important, as it may help to link up that small but anomalous group of cave paintings belonging to the northern style that appears in the extreme south-west of the country (for example, at the cave of La Pileta, etc.). These cave paintings have no affinities with those of eastern Spain, and their situation presents some difficulties. But while most of the country was probably Capsian in culture, there may have been a certain filtration of the more northerly cultures southwards along the coast.

It is impossible to determine the motives underlying the production of the eastern Spanish art. Certainly the paintings were not mere decorations for home sites, and this is obvious when it is remembered that hearths and tools have hardly ever been discovered when excavations have been made in the painted rock-shelters. The explanation which so admirably accounts for the cave paintings in France and northern Spain cannot hold here, as the paintings are always found in broad daylight. In one instance at Cantos de la Visera a well-drawn bull in light red has been painted over at a later date in chocolate and altered into a stag. The later drawing is far inferior to the earlier, but why the artist should take the trouble to destroy a previously drawn animal and replace it in an inferior manner by the figure

[1] Perhaps, rather, a sort of Aterian. See Note, page 158.

of another kind of beast is of course completely inexplicable. It seems to indicate, however, that the figures had some meaning and were perhaps of importance to the folk who lived at that time. While frequently painted rock-shelters (e.g. Alpéra) are prominent for miles around and command an excellent view, this is by no means invariably the case and there are plenty of localities which are neither prominent nor particularly outstanding. It can only be suggested that possibly they were meeting places where different families or tribes collected for various purposes, and that as these meeting places were specially set apart they were decorated. The decoration was not simply a beautification of the site, however, as is obvious when we consider how often the paintings are drawn overlapping one another with little reference to what was there before. Admittedly this explanation is far from satisfactory, but prehistorians have nothing better to offer until further discoveries throw fresh light on the problem.

Chapter XIV

FIELD WORK

NO amount of reading is really a substitute for practical experience, and no amount of theoretical study about how to explore can ever take the place of actual work in the field. At the same time a few hints as to how the student should set about various kinds of field work and the sort of things for which he should look out may not be out of place. Roughly speaking, the possible kinds of investigation that may present themselves fall into three categories: (i) cave or rock-shelter sites, (ii) open stations, or (iii) settlement sites. A few notes will be given on each of these, together with a few remarks on the subsequent treatment of any finds.

CAVE OR ROCK-SHELTER SITES. As a preliminary it may be stated at once that no one without previous experience should attempt this sort of exploration unaccompanied by some competent excavator. Almost certainly irreparable damage would be done to the site, not from any want of trouble on the part of the novice, but simply as the result of lack of knowledge whereby precious information which might have been obtained in the course of the dig would fail to be noted and would therefore be irretrievably lost. Whereas there are innumerable open settlement sites in gravel beds, and other similar localities where industries occur, comparatively speaking there are only a few cave sites known and it is by no means certain that further exploration will vastly increase this number. The next generation, then, will reasonably curse the inexperienced amateur of to-day if he has "hogged" one of the few places where important evidence about early man could have been collected. If for any reason, however, it be decided that an excavation in a cave or rock-shelter is advisable, the following notes may not be unhelpful.

A rock-shelter or home-site in a cave mouth, as a rule, consists of two parts; the shelter proper and the terrace in front of it. Excavation in both may yield prehistoric industries. To begin with, a narrow trench should be dug inwards through the terrace to the back wall of the rock-shelter, and secondly, another at right angles along the length of the terrace. These trial trenches should be carefully excavated, as far as possible in layers, each layer being not more than 6 to 9 in. thick; and the contents of any interest from each should be carefully kept separate and packed up before a fresh layer is excavated. When the soil is very powdery and trenches with more or less vertical walls are impossible, a certain amount of shoring up is often advisable. As a result of studying the sides of the trenches, the investigator can obtain an idea of the stratigraphy of the place, and the finds made from different layers will enable him to determine what sort of industries, belonging to what cultures, occur at the site. Should there be no stratigraphy, and should the industry be uniform from top to bottom, the matter is now simple: it is merely a question of careful excavation of the whole of the site and the collection of any specimens which are found. Should, however, the walls of the trenches clearly indicate that a number of distinct layers occur, in stratigraphical sequence perhaps slightly differing from each other in colour or constitution, and should the industries indicate that people of different cultures inhabited the rock-shelter at different times, then very great care must be taken before further excavation is attempted. Especially troublesome is the case where no obvious stratigraphy exists, and no distinct layers can be seen, the whole rock-shelter filling being uniform in colour and texture, yet the finds showing variations from top to bottom. Then indeed the excavation requires a prehistorian trained for the job!

Consider first the case where a definite stratigraphy can be made out. Layer by layer the cave infilling must be removed, keeping as far as possible to the indications given by the stratigraphy. It should be remembered that the various layers in a rock-shelter are by no means always horizontal. There may have been a large boulder or other obstruction on the floor of the shelter over which the layers curve, so that here they will be neither horizontal nor necessarily of uniform thickness, and therefore the industry contained in any one layer will not be found at exactly the same level throughout the site. Nothing but experience and common-sense can help the excavator. In the last case, where there is no obvious stratigraphy but more than one industry is present, a sort of dead reckoning, such as was used in making the trial trenches, has to be employed and uniform layers some 6 to 9 in. thick removed, specially great attention being now paid to the industries found, as a typological study of them, while the excavation is in progress, may enable the investigator to develop for himself a sort of stratigraphy.

Throughout the excavation, where the deposits have not been sealed in by such material as stalagmite, the excavator must be on the look out for traces of burrowing animals, who tend to make a "salad" of the deposits.

As an example of their destructive work one may cite the Victoria Cave near Settle which was excavated with meticulous care in the latter half of the last century. The exact position of every specimen was carefully marked and the whole was done with the highest skill then practised. But subsequent investigation of the site shows that the bottom layer is not horizontal but rises rapidly towards the back of the cave, and that the upper layers are bedded against it. It only required horizontal movement, therefore, to bring objects from the earlier layers into the later ones, and as the whole site is riddled with rabbit holes any stratigraphical evidence adduced from it is worthless. Bones, cut with a metal tool, were discovered deep down in a pre-glacial layer, while the remains of a prehistoric fauna occurred with Romano-British enamels. The rabbit is the deadly enemy of prehistorians!

For careful excavation a small stout broad-bladed knife is the best weapon unless the deposit is too hard. Of course it sometimes happens where a layer is practically stalagmite that dynamite has to be employed, but obviously no amateur should attempt the blowing up of a layer unless he has had previous experience, since naturally any contained industry is likely to be destroyed in the process. Larger objects can readily be collected by hand and placed in boxes, but before the earth is finally tipped away it should be put through two riddles of varying size. In this way many small artifacts that might have been missed can be collected. In passing it might be mentioned that riddling is only possible when the earth is dry and it is sometimes necessary to hold up an excavation for several days to allow this process to take place. It sometimes happens, too, incidentally, that, when dry, any stratification that exists may show up more clearly than when the whole deposit is wet.

Stone implements can be readily picked out; bones, being more fragile, have often to be carefully detached with a penknife. Where bones of human beings are suspected even this method should not be straight away attempted. Indeed, once again it cannot be too strongly urged that, especially if human remains are found, experts should be called in and nothing done until their arrival, except the taking of detailed photographs of the site. If bones occur in soft damp earth their consistency is frequently like that of a madeira cake. In this case they can sometimes be hardened by painting them over with shellac dissolved in methylated spirit—about 1 lb. of brown shellac dissolved in 1½ pints of spirit. The bones may have to be treated many times and it may be several days before they are hard enough to make it safe for further excavation to take place around them. As the portion exposed hardens up, more and more excavation can take place and fresh portions of the bones be treated. In very bad places actual injection of the shellac into the bones may be necessary. When the bones are very dry and crumbly they should not be treated with shellac but with gelatine —1 lb. gelatine to 1½ pints of boiling water—the same procedure as before being adopted. When the bones have been sufficiently hardened to permit of their being fully exposed, careful photographs should be taken and the explorer, before he proceeds further, should be sure that these show everything really well. It is no good being told afterwards that unfortunately owing to failure in exposure the results are poor. The photographs can never be taken again. The removal of the bones can take place either separately or, if they still remain fragile, the whole block of earth in which they occur may have to be cut out. This latter business involves the isolation and under-pinning of a large mass of material and for this purpose it is sometimes useful to swaddle as it were the whole thing in strips of calico carefully washed and then dipped in plaster of Paris. The contained block can then be removed as a sort of mummy, boxed, and taken to a laboratory for subsequent examination.

It may be noted in passing that while skeletons may occur anywhere, they are more frequently found close to the back wall of the rock-shelter.

Little more can be said as to excavations in a cave or rock-shelter site.[1] Most of the difficulties are connected with the stratigraphy and this of course cannot be re-examined when the site has once been dug. Innumerable photographs should be taken at various stages, as these will be useful for reference and may help to settle any points in dispute which may subsequently arise. Should paintings or engravings occur, these must, of course, be traced and if possible photographed. Careful manipulation of the illumination, whether artificial or not, will often make the drawings show up much more clearly. In certain cases, too, they show up much more distinctly if very carefully damped.

OPEN STATIONS. Most of the open sites of palaeolithic age likely to be investigated by the ordinary student occur in gravel or brick-earth pits. Whereas in cave or rock-shelter sites the investigator is chiefly concerned with the determination of the cultural stratigraphy, in gravel or brick-earth beds he is more occupied with the geological problems of the different layers

[1] Of course maps of the site and sections should be drawn and a careful record kept of where all the finds occurred.

present. To begin with, the account of the district (as given in the *Memoirs of H.M. Geological Survey*) should be consulted and, if possible, the local geology determined. Let us take for example a newly opened gravel pit which has yielded coups-de-poing. When such a site is visited the investigator should start by examining a clean section as free as possible from talus. Photographs should be taken and a sketch of the various deposits made, both the photographs and the sketch being labelled not only with the name of the locality but also with the date, as such sections, of course, rapidly disappear. An attempt should next be made to answer the following questions. Is there only one deposit visible, or is there clearly a stratigraphical sequence of several layers each showing different characteristics? In the latter case do the various layers rest evenly on one another or is there any geological unconformity between them? Frequently in the south and east of England the bottom layers in a gravel pit will be found to be evenly bedded, while the upper layers will be twisted and contorted, almost invariably as a result of solifluxion. Were the various deposits laid down by water action, that is are the contained pebbles rounded and evenly bedded, or are they angular with sharp edges and jumbled together anyhow, the whole deposit being perhaps an outwash gravel from some quaternary glacier? If it is decided that the gravels are of fluviatile origin, are they a river terrace gravel or not, and if so which? Is the river terrace connected with the present river valley system or not? The archeological importance of the answers to these questions will, of course, be obvious.

Next, if possible, implements should be collected from the different layers. But unfortunately it is very rare, unless the site happens to be a particularly rich

one, that such *in situ* finds are made. It is more usual
for the tools to be collected by workmen when riddling
the gravel and it is then usually too late to ascertain
definitely from what layer they came. However, in this
connection a very careful study of the state of preservation and patina of the finds will sometimes, as has
been indicated (p. 56), enable the prehistorian to be
fairly certain whence came the artifacts.

SETTLEMENT SITES. Settlement sites of palaeolithic
age are more than rare and the following suggestions
perhaps rather refer to explorations of neolithic date.
A good plan is to select a point just outside what is
considered to be the margin of a site; fix the position
as accurately as possible on the best available large scale
map of the district and drive in a peg, labelling it
"A". From A stretch a measure or string marked off
in yards and feet (it is often convenient to tie little
knots of red cotton at every yard and black cotton at
every foot when a string and not a measure is used)
over the part of the site to be excavated. See that this
cord is securely attached to another peg, labelled "B",
and that it is both straight and level. For this purpose
a spirit level is necessary, the pegs A and B being
raised or lowered respectively until as horizontal a line
as possible is obtained. The level line A–B then forms
the datum to which everything found is referred, and
its exact position can be readily plotted on a large scale
map of the district should one exist. Of course A–B
should not be too long. A trench is next opened alongside A–B either to the right or left about 1 yard wide,
layers of some 9 inches or so thick being excavated at
a time. Every important object found should be referred
to A–B—so many yards and feet along A–B, so much

to its right or left, and so far below it. The result can
be reduced to a formula which can be written on the
object thus:

A 3′ 6″   R 15″   D 1′ 9″,

meaning: 3½ ft. along A–B, 15 in. to its right and
1 ft. 9 in. below it. Later, of course, other trenches
can be opened as desired, objects found being still
referred to A–B. By this simple means the position
of all important objects can be marked and the whole
excavation if necessary reconstructed afterwards in the
laboratory. The single datum line method can also be
employed when excavating burial mounds and so on,
but for this purpose other methods are more usual.
But as they are of little use to the palaeolithic prehistorian, their study is outside the domain of this book.

SUBSEQUENT TREATMENT OF FINDS. It cannot be
too strongly urged on all investigators in the field that
no time should be lost in labelling their specimens.
For this purpose it is not enough merely to shove them
together in a box with a paper label on the top. Acci-
dents occur, and a mixture of the industries results.
Each specimen should have a pencil hieroglyphic of
some sort written on it, while one or two of the bigger
and finer specimens should have the full name of the
locality indicated too. Nor is it enough nowadays merely
to label the finds as having been collected in such and
such a parish; as far as possible the exact field, or even
part of the field, or the exact layer in the pit, should
be marked. It is advisable not to wash specimens too
carefully but to leave a certain amount of the material
in which they occurred in the interstices. Should argument as to the exact original position of a specimen
subsequently arise, the matter can frequently be settled

by microscopic examination of the material still adhering to it and a comparison of this with the constitution of layers still to be seen in the pit. It does not mean that a specimen must be left covered with dirt, merely that sufficient evidence as to its original surroundings should be preserved. The treatment of any bones which may happen to be discovered has already been described.

It cannot be too strongly urged that the investigator in the field has two things to do: (i) to collect specimens and (ii) to note all details in connection with their environment and occurrence.

Elaborate field notes should therefore always be made as it is never possible subsequently to obtain this information. The circumstances under which the finds occur are often as important to the prehistorian as the finds themselves.

Chapter XV

EPILOGUE

IN Europe the Old Stone Age was replaced by cultures of the mesolithic epoch. I have described these in some detail in another book, so will here only give a few notes about the story of man's development from a mere food gatherer to a food producer.

The dawn of the mesolithic epoch coincides with profound change in our climatic conditions. Pleistocene (quaternary) times are over and the holocene period of the fifth and current volume of geological time begins. Climate changes still happen during this period and are important, but no longer do we have great alterations in temperature. The alternations are now as much due to changes in humidity, and we have to deal with the different types of forest trees growing in a given region rather than with advances and retreats of ice sheets and solifluxion effects in gravel beds.

The cultures of this epoch are numerous and somewhat monotonous. Naturally they are stemmed in the earlier palaeolithic, but in their later phases, new ideas penetrating from outside profoundly changed man's way of life, already modified by the different physical and weather conditions under which he had to live. The earliest of these immediately post-palaeolithic cultures—found near Hamburg and elsewhere—is connected in part with cultures whose industries are characterised by the occurrence of small shouldered points. Somewhat similar industries occur as far away as Poland (Swiderian) where they have been found beneath very ancient dunes. But the chief mesolithic cultures are the Tardenoisian, Azilian, and Asturian in the southern half of the Continent, and the Maglemosean, Campignian and Kitchen Midden in the north. The Tardenoisian is characterised by the presence of innumerable pigmy flints including the micro-burin type.[1] Bone tools are very rare, and there is no art of any kind.

[1] It does not concern us here to discuss whether the micro-burin is an intentional tool-form or, as is more likely, merely a by-product in the manufacture of other pigmy tools. It remains for prehistorians a very characteristic object.

Clearly the Tardenoisians had discovered the advantages of the composite tool. As soft-wood forests then abounded presumably the hafts were made of wood. The Azilian culture shows some Magdalenian influence, and in fact is found in areas where the Magdalenians formerly reigned supreme. Possibly the Tardenoisians under Magdalenian influence developed the characteristic Azilian industries with harpoons, painted pebbles, small round scrapers, angle burins, etc.? The Asturian is of minor importance, being confined mainly to the north-west of Spain and of Portugal. The Maglemosean, the chief culture of the northern province, differs profoundly from the Tardenoisian. Whereas the latter was probably evolved from late developments of our western European Aurignacian complex, the former may owe its origin to the late palaeolithic of Central Europe. There are rich stone and bone industries, and also antler sleeves for hafting stone tools (adzes, etc.). Many of the bone objects are decorated with geometric designs. The Campignian and Kitchen Midden cultures show a great falling off from Maglemosean standards, but now clearer evidence of neolithic influence is appearing. There is little doubt that late mesolithic man had already acquired some simple agricultural knowledge, that he had to some extent become "neolithicised". Very occasionally towards the top of the Kitchen Midden deposits—those great heaps of shells and dust-bin rubbish so common in Denmark—some pottery is found and an occasional polished tool.

The arrival of the full neolithic epoch is marked by the four new discoveries which profoundly changed the whole human way of life: man had learnt to practise agriculture, to domesticate animals, to make pottery and to grind and polish his stone tools. Any long discussion about where and how these discoveries were made is obviously outside the scope of a brief epilogue, but their effects were so far-reaching that a few words will not be out of place. The origin of the neolithic civilisation may have been single or multiple, it may have sprung from a single cradle or from several. Perhaps an area once fertile but becoming dry, wnere oasis conditions obtained, would be one in which man would begin to realise that something new must be attempted if he was to survive. His thus sharpened intelligence would notice the growth of accidentally spilled wild grain, and the results of the mating of wild animals, which had perhaps been caught when young and tamed. However that may have been, humanity now for the first time became not independent of Nature, we are not entirely independent of her to-day, but less immediately at her mercy. Now there were stocks of grain and home-reared animals to even out seasonal deficiencies in the natural food supply. Also more food was thus available and in consequence the population no doubt rapidly increased. A given area of country can only support a very limited hunting population but a much denser farming one—for among really primitive folk Malthus' Law does more or less hold good. But it was agriculture particularly that changed man's mode of life. For the first time villages sprang up and a simple form of community life emerged. Not everyone would have to spend his whole time in collecting food in order to live. Specialisation became possible, some tilled the soil, others looked after the animals, others made the various necessary tools, others protected the community. For with communal property came danger from other less provident groups who had wasted their stores in riotous living! But with the rise of community life man has to face a new-old problem now appearing for the first time in human history. Man (or woman) has to learn to live in close contact with his fellows. Customs necessary for the very existence of any human polity, however primitive, have to be evolved, for no group can long survive whose members freely lie, steal, murder, etc. As the communities increased in size and importance the problem arose of how to enforce these customs in days when no centralised police force had been thought of—a problem to become more acute in the Near East as a veritable urban life developed in the Bronze Age. Among the early (Aryan) inhabitants of the region between the upper Euphrates and Tigris—the Mitanni—investigators have traced the growth of the concept of a god of cosmic and social order, whose interest was the upholding of community life and who punished wrong doers. This is a very different idea to that of cave magic practised to secure or increase the natural food supply. The small neolithic communities were doubtless very primitive and simple, but the germ of our own civilisation was there. Our own way of life and thought evolved from these early village settlements; it could never have come directly from the cave men of the Old Stone Age.

The discovery of pottery making refined the home and allowed for the making of many useful objects. The grinding and polishing technique for tool making permitted carpentry for the first time. A flint when knapped gives a sharp but brittle edge. Even a fine-grained rock, comprising as it does minerals of varying hardnesses and cleavage planes, cannot yield a sharp edge by the knapping process, though such materials allow a tough one to be produced. But the grinding and polishing technique does permit a high degree of sharpness coupled with toughness, and this is just what is required for working in wood.

So we say good-bye to our Old Stone Age folk and welcome in the New Stone Age, soon to pass on into the Metal Age. Humanity has lived a very long time on this globe, and progress has been very variable both in time and place, sometimes seeming to leap forward and at other times almost to turn back to repeat its efforts. But progress is spiral, not merely circular, there are three, not two, dimensions to consider. History indeed repeats itself—but with a difference each time, and in the cyclic turns of material progress can we not trace a gentle, just discernible gleam of higher progression, which in spite of apparent set-backs all the time does sometimes let us see that man is ever moving away from the unselfconscious life of his animal forbears towards a higher, finer way of existence?

BIBLIOGRAPHY

IT is not suggested that the following is, in any sense, a complete bibliography of the Old Stone Age, and the absence of any particular work is no indication of its little importance. Quite clearly, however, students wishing to go more deeply into the subject must have some indication where to delve next.

General Works dealing with the subject as a whole.

Apes and Men; Hunters and Artists. Vols. I and II of the "Corridors of Time" Series, by Harold Peake and Hubert John Fleure (Clarendon Press, 1927).

Man the Tool-maker, 2nd ed., by Kenneth P. Oakley (British Museum, Natural History, 1950).

Tools and the Man, by W. B. Wright (G. Bell and Sons, 1939).

Adam's Ancestors, 4th ed., by L. S. B. Leakey (Methuen and Co., 1953).

Prehistory, 2nd ed., by M. C. Burkitt (Cambridge University Press, 1925).

Fossil Man in Spain, by Hugo Obermaier (Oxford University Press, 1924).

Prelude to History, by Adrian Coates (Methuen and Co., 1951).

A Hundred Years of Archaeology, by G. E. Daniel (Duckworth and Co., 1950).

Books specially concerned with Great Britain.

The Antiquity of Man in East Anglia, by Reid Moir (Cambridge University Press, 1927).

The Upper Palaeolithic Age in Britain, by D. A. E. Garrod (Oxford University Press, 1926).

Ancient Stone Implements of Great Britain, 2nd ed. by Sir John Evans (Longmans, Green and Co., 1897).

The last-mentioned book is a classic and still contains some useful information as to distribution, etc. which is not readily obtainable elsewhere.

Quaternary Geology.

Books on this subject are innumerable, but two important ones are:

The Quaternary Ice Age, 2nd ed., by W. B. Wright (Macmillan and Co., 1937).
Dating the Past, 2nd ed., by F. E. Zeuner (Methuen and Co., 1950).

Palaeolithic Art.

The classic works of reference for students wishing to study the Cave Art in France or Spain have appeared from time to time for the most part under the auspices of the Institut de Paléontologie Humaine and they include the following volumes:

> *La Caverne d'Altamira.* (New edition.)
> *La Caverne de Font-de-Gaume.*
> *Les Cavernes de la Région Cantabrique.*
> *La Pasiéga.*
> *La Pileta.*
> *Les Combarelles.*

In each case the work is chiefly due to the Abbé H. Breuil.

Other useful works are the following:

The Art of the Cave Dweller, by G. Baldwin Brown (John Murray, 1928).
Prehistoric Painting, by Alan H. Brodrick (Avalon Press, 1948).
Lascaux, a Commentary, by Alan H. Brodrick (Lindsay Drummond, 1949).
The Lascaux Cave Paintings, by Fernand Windels (Faber and Faber, 1949).
Quatre Cents Siècles d'Art Pariétal, by Abbé H. Breuil (Centre d'Études.... Préhistoriques, Montignac-sur-Vézère, Dordogne, 1952).
Art in the Ice Age, by J. Maringer and H. G. Bandi (Allen and Unwin, 1953).

As regards the home art there is a very fine volume of reproductions of objects found in the Pyrenees in a corpus of plates entitled,

L'Art pendant l'Âge du Renne, by Édouard Piette (Masson et Cie, 1907).

Outlined sketches of a large number of paintings and engravings both from the caves and the homes can be seen in two inexpensive works, exceedingly useful as small books of reference:

Répertoire de l'Art quaternaire, by the late Salomon Reinach (Ernest Leroux, Paris).

L'Art Préhistorique, by the late Comte de Saint-Périer (Les Éditions Rieder, Paris, 1932).

Periodicals which constantly contain information of importance and which should be followed by students are the following (except in the case of ' L'Anthropologie' only English periodicals are given):

L'Anthropologie. Paris (Masson et Cie).

Antiquity. Edited by O. G. S. Crawford (John Bellows, Gloucester).

The Antiquaries' Journal. (Oxford University Press.)

Journal of the Royal Anthropological Institute and *Man*. Containing many ethnological as well as prehistoric papers.

The Proceedings of the Prehistoric Society (John Bellows, Gloucester).

Books on certain areas and periods adjoining those dealt with in this volume.

The Stone Age Cultures of South Africa, by A. J. H. Goodwin and C. van Riet Lowe (*Annals of the South African Museum*, vol. XXVII, 1929).

South Africa's Past in Stone and Paint, by M. C. Burkitt (Cambridge University Press, 1928).

The Stone Age Cultures of Kenya Colony, by L. S. B. Leakey (Cambridge University Press, 1931).

The Prehistoric Archaeology of North West Africa, by F. R. Wulsin (Cambridge, Mass. 1941).

Kharga Oasis in Prehistory, by G. Caton-Thompson (University of London Athlone Press, 1952).

The Stone Age of Mount Carmel, by D. A. E. Garrod and D. M. A. Bate (Oxford, Clarendon Press, 1937).

The Mesolithic Age in Britain, by J. G. D. Clark (Cambridge University Press, 1932).

The Mesolithic Settlement of Northern Europe, by J. G. D. Clark (Cambridge University Press, 1936).

Our Early Ancestors, an Introductory Study of Mesolithic, Neolithic and Copper Age Cultures in Europe and Adjacent Regions, by M. C. Burkitt (Cambridge University Press, 1926).

The Irish Stone Age, by H. L. Movius (Cambridge University Press, 1942).

The Dawn of European Civilization, 4th ed., by Prof. V. G. Childe (Kegan Paul, 1947).

The Prehistoric Foundations of Europe, by C. F. C. Hawkes (Methuen, 1940).

Fossil Man.

Important books which should be consulted for descriptions of the finds of prehistoric human remains are:

Les Hommes Fossiles, 3rd ed., by Marcellin Boule (Masson et Cie., Paris, 1946).

The Antiquity of Man, 2nd ed., by Sir Arthur Keith (Williams and Norgate, 1925).

New Discoveries Relating to the Antiquity of Man, by Sir Arthur Keith (Williams and Norgate, 1931).

Early Man, by A. H. Brodrick (Hutchinson's Scientific and Technical Publications, 1948).

Mankind So Far, by W. W. Howells (Zigma Book Co. Ltd., 1947).

Up from the Ape, by E. A. Hooton (Macmillan, 1948).

INDEX